Surveys + Resource Mapping
Min. Environment
Bob Howie
August 86 Victoria

To Gary Runka
all Love
Jan 19/87

CONSERVING SOIL

INSIGHTS FROM SOCIOECONOMIC RESEARCH

CONSERVING SOIL

INSIGHTS
FROM SOCIOECONOMIC
RESEARCH

Stephen B. Lovejoy
Ted L. Napier
Editors

Published for
North Central Regional Research Committee 162,
Socioeconomic Factors Affecting the Adoption
of Soil Conservation Practices
by the
Soil Conservation Society of America
7515 Northeast Ankeny Road
Ankeny, Iowa 50021

$8.00

Library of Congress Cataloging in Publication Data

Main entry under title:

Conserving soil.

Based on papers presented at a symposium, held June 3-5, 1985, at Zion, Illinois.
Includes index.
1. Land use, Rural—Government policy—United States—Congresses. 2. Soil conservation—Government policy—United States—Congresses. I. Lovejoy, Stephen B. II. Napier, Ted L. III. Socioeconomic Factors Affecting the Adoption of Soil Conservation Practices (U.S.) North Central Regional Research Committee 162. IV. Soil Conservation Society of America.
HD256.C64 1986   333.76'16'0973   86-1752
ISBN 0-935734-12-0

The Soil Conservation Society of America, founded in 1945, is a nonprofit scientific and educational association dedicated to advancing the science and art of good land use. Its 13,000 members worldwide include researchers, administrators, educators, planners, managers, and technicians with a profound interest in the wise use of land and water resources. Most academic disciplines concerned with the management of land and water resources are represented.

Opinions, interpretations, and conclusions expressed in this book are those of the authors.

This book is based on material presented at a symposium, "Soil and Water Conservation: Implications of Social and Economic Research for Policy Development and Program Implementation," held June 3-5, 1985, at Illinois Beach State Park, Zion, Illinois. That symposium and this book were sponsored by the North Central Regional Research Committee 162, Socioeconomic Factors Affecting the Adoption of Soil Conservation Practices, with the financial support of the Soil Conservation Service, U.S. Department of Agriculture; Resources for the Future, Inc.; Natural Resource Economics Division, Economic Research Service, U.S. Department of Agriculture; and the Farm Foundation.

North Central Regional Research Committee 162

Socioeconomic Factors Affecting the Adoption of Soil Conservation Practices

Chairman
Stephen B. Lovejoy
Department of Agricultural Economics
Purdue University

Secretary
Ted L. Napier
Department of Agricultural Economics
and Rural Sociology
The Ohio State University

Gordon L. Bultena
Department of Sociology
Iowa State University

John E. Carlson
Department of Agricultural Economics
University of Idaho

David E. Ervin
Department of Agricultural Economics
University of Missouri-Columbia

Jerald J. Fletcher
Department of Agricultural Economics
Purdue University

William Heffernan
Department of Rural Sociology
University of Missouri-Columbia

H. Douglas Jose
Department of Agricultural Economics
University of Nebraska-Lincoln

Steven E. Kraft
Department of Agribusiness Economics
Southern Illinois University

William Alex McIntosh
Department of Rural Sociology
Texas A&M University

Edgar L. Michalson
Department of Agricultural Economics
University of Idaho

Andrew Sofranko
Department of Agricultural Economics
University of Illinois

Louis E. Swanson
Department of Sociology
University of Kentucky

Cameron S. Thraen
Department of Agricultural Economics
and Rural Sociology
The Ohio State University

John Van Es
Department of Agricultural Economics
University of Illinois

Administrative Advisor
Harvey J. Schweitzer
Department of Agricultural Economics
University of Illinois

Contents

Preface xi

I. The Institutional Environment

1 Why Soil Erosion: A Social Science Perspective
Sandra S. Batie 3

2 Macro-economics of Soil Conservation
John A. Miranowski 15

3 Soil and Water Conservation: A Farm Structural
and Public Policy Context
Frederick H. Buttel and Louis E. Swanson 26

4 Interorganizational Relations in Conservation
Targeting Programs
James Nielson 40

II. Information Needs and Dissemination

5 Information Needs for Conservation Decisions
Jerald J. Fletcher and Wesley D. Seitz 55

6 Sources of Information and Technical Assistance
for Farmers in Controlling Soil Erosion
Gordon L. Bultena and Eric O. Hoiberg 71

7 Early Adopters and Nonusers of No-till in the
Pacific Northwest: A Comparison
John E. Carlson and Don A. Dillman 83

III. Constraints to Conservation

8   Constraints to Practicing Soil Conservation: Land
    Tenure Relationships
    David E. Ervin   95

9   Barriers to Adoption of Soil Conservation
    Practices on Farms
    Louis E. Swanson, Silvana M. Camboni, and
    Ted L. Napier   108

10 Integration of Social and Physical Analysis: The
    Potential for Micro-targeting
    Stephen B. Lovejoy, John Gary Lee, and
    David B. Beasley   121

IV. Implications for Policy Development and Program Implementation

11 The Socioeconomic Dimensions of Soil and Water
    Conservation: Some Reaction
    Richard Duesterhaus   133
    Peter M. Tidd   135
    Don Paarlberg   136
    C. Oran Little   138

12 The Socioeconomic Dimensions of Soil and Water
    Conservation: Some Discussion

    Micro and Macro Factors Influencing the Adoption
    of Soil and Water Conservation Practices
    Cameron S. Thraen, Ted L. Napier, and
    James A. Maetzold   140

    Information Needs and Dissemination
    Steven E. Kraft, William Alex McIntosh, and
    Edgar Michalson   143

    Constraints to Conservation
    Thomas J. Hoban IV, Eric Hoiberg, and
    Barbara Osgood   146

    Index   151

Contributors

SANDRA S. BATIE, Professor
Department of Agricultural Economics, Virginia Polytechnic Institute and State University, Blacksburg

DAVID B. BEASLEY, Associate Professor
Department of Agricultural Engineering, Purdue University, West Lafayette, Indiana

GORDON L. BULTENA, Professor
Department of Sociology and Anthropology, Iowa State University, Ames

FREDERICK H. BUTTEL, Associate Professor
Department of Rural Sociology, Cornell University, Ithaca, New York

SILVANA M. CAMBONI, Development Officer
Ohio State University Research Foundation, Columbus

JOHN E. CARLSON, Professor
Department of Agricultural Economics, University of Idaho, Boise

DON A. DILLMAN, Professor
Department of Rural Sociology, Washington State University, Pullman

RICHARD DUESTERHAUS, Assistant Chief
Soil Conservation Service, U.S. Department of Agriculture, Washington, D.C.

DAVID E. ERVIN, Associate Professor
Department of Agricultural Economics, University of Missouri, Columbia

JERALD J. FLETCHER, Assistant Professor
Department of Agricultural Economics, Purdue University, West Lafayette, Indiana

THOMAS J. HOBAN IV, Research Assistant
Department of Sociology and Anthropology, Iowa State University, Ames

ERIC HOIBERG, Associate Professor
Department of Sociology and Anthropology, Iowa State University, Ames

STEVEN E. KRAFT, Assistant Professor
Department of Agribusiness Economics, Southern Illinois University, Carbondale

JOHN GARY LEE, Graduate Assistant
Department of Agricultural Economics, Purdue University, West Lafayette, Indiana

C. ORAN LITTLE, Associate Dean
Kentucky Agricultural Experiment Station, University of Kentucky, Lexington

STEPHEN B. LOVEJOY, Associate Professor
Department of Agricultural Economics, Purdue University, West Lafayette, Indiana

JAMES A. MAETZOLD, Economist
Appraisal and Program Development, Soil Conservation Service, U.S. Department of
Agriculture, Washington, D.C.

WILLIAM ALEX MCINTOSH, Associate Professor
Department of Rural Sociology, Texas A&M University, College Station

EDGAR MICHALSON, Professor
Department of Agricultural Economics, University of Idaho, Moscow

JOHN A MIRANOWSKI, Director
Natural Resource Economics Division, Economic Research Service, U.S. Department of
Agriculture, Washington, D.C.

TED L. NAPIER, Professor
Department of Agricultural Economics and Rural Sociology, Ohio State University,
Columbus

JAMES NIELSON, Project Leader (retired)
Agricultural Research Service, U.S. Department of Agriculture, Seattle, Washington

BARBARA OSGOOD, National Sociologist
Economics and Social Sciences Division, Soil Conservation Service, U.S. Department of
Agriculture, Washington, D.C.

DON PAARLBERG, Professor Emeritus
Department of Agricultural Economics, Purdue University, West Lafayette, Indiana

WESLEY D. SEITZ, Professor and Head
Department of Agricultural Economics, University of Illinois, Urbana

LOUIS E. SWANSON, Assistant Professor
Department of Sociology, University of Kentucky, Lexington

PETER M. TIDD, Director
Appraisal and Program Development, Soil Conservation Service, U.S. Department of
Agriculture, Washington, D.C.

CAMERON S. THRAEN, Assistant Professor
Department of Agricultural Economics and Rural Sociology, Ohio State University,
Columbus

Preface

Conservationists have long sought the ultimate technology for protecting the land from soil erosion. Of late, however, many conservation professionals have come to realize that government policies, the way in which programs are implemented, and human behavior are often as important as technology. More emphasis has been given to policy development and the implementation of conservation programs as a result.

Methods exist to control soil erosion and to protect soil and water resources. Agricultural scientists have known about these methods for decades. But many of the technologies and farming practices advocated by agricultural scientists are not used by farmers and ranchers in the United States. Why? Some researchers question the applicability of the technologies. Others suggest the lack of adoption is a result of conflicting government policies or inadequate conservation programs.

Another way of looking at this issue is to realize that technology is a necessary condition for conserving soil but not a sufficient condition. Most people now recognize the importance of access to information, the role of institutions, and the barriers to the wise use of soil and water resources. Social scientists, responding to this recognition, have initiated research on many of the behavioral aspects of soil conservation.

One group of social scientists in the north central region of the United States met in the early 1980s to discuss the commonalities of their research and design strategies for coordinating those efforts. As a result of the interest demonstrated by these scientists, a north central regional research project, "Socioeconomic Factors Affecting the Adoption of Soil Conservation Practices" (NC-162), came into being. The activities of this project ultimately led to a national symposium, "Soil and Water Conservation: Implications of Social and Economic Research for Policy Development and Program Implementation," held June 3-5, 1985, in Zion, Illinois.

A major purpose of the symposium was to examine the state of the art in socioeconomic research on soil conservation to determine why many farmers do not adopt erosion control practices. The focus of the symposium was on three broad areas of concern:

1. Effects of institutional environments on conservation behavior, including the effects of macro-economic and macro-social factors, factors related to the structure of agriculture, and the impacts of interorganizational relationships.

2. Types of information needed to make conservation decisions and the way that sources of information affect conservation behavior.

3. Social and institutional barriers to the adoption of conservation practices.

The book presents the main issues addressed by the presenters at the symposium. It also presents the reactions of a selected panel of conservation professionals and summaries of discussion-group sessions attended by symposium participants. The audience represented a broad range of individuals from agriculture. Most participants had some association with conservation programs. Those attending included representatives from agribusinesses, agricultural interest groups, universities, the Soil Conservation Service, the U.S. Department of the Interior, the U.S. Environmental Protection Agency, state conservation agencies, and the Cooperative Extension Service.

We would like to take this opportunity to thank the many people who contributed to the success of the symposium, the synopsis published earlier, and this volume. Funding to support these efforts were received from the Soil Conservation Service (U.S. Department of Agriculture), the National Center for Food and Agricultural Policy (Resources for the Future), the Natural Resource Economics Division of the Economic Research Service (USDA), and the Farm Foundation. The many hours expended by members of the NC-162 committee are gratefully acknowledged. The support of the universities and the directors of the agricultural experiment stations was essential for the formation and functioning of the committee. Lastly, we acknowledge the significant contribution of Max Schnepf and the Soil Conservation Society of America in making this volume possible.

Stephen B. Lovejoy
Ted L. Napier

I
The Institutional Environment

1

Why Soil Erosion: A Social Science Perspective

Sandra S. Batie

The National Resource Inventories of 1977 and 1982 for the first time provided a statistically valid picture of the magnitude and location of soil erosion in the United States. According to the 1977 inventory, estimated water-caused erosion on cropland was 1.9 million tons; wind erosion on cropland was .9 million tons. The inventories revealed further that erosion on cropland is highly concentrated. Almost 87 percent of the 1977 cropland did not erode at rates considered excessive (over 5 tons per acre per year). Or, viewed differently, 5 percent of the cropland acreage accounted for 36 percent of the total erosion and 66 percent of the excessive erosion.

These erosion rates are associated with two types of damages: on-farm losses in soil productivity and off-farm air and water pollution. Studies indicate, for example, that erosion can lower yields on many soils. If erosion has reduced the soil's water-holding capacity, the rooting depth available to the plant, or the water infiltration rate, adding fertilizer may not offset the yield-reducing effects.

Erosion also affects air and water quality. Agriculture is considered the main source for that part of the nation's water pollution that comes from diffuse (nonpoint) sources. Soil particles in water runoff carry along fertilizer residues, pesticides, dissolved minerals (such as salts), and animal wastes (with associated bacteria).

Such damages do not imply that there are no technologically feasible solutions. Farmers can choose among many soil conservation techniques, such as changing the characteristics of a field's topography with terraces, planting only the least erodible land, rotating crops, stripcropping, planting on the contour, retaining crop residues on the field surface after harvesting, constructing waterways, or using such methods as no-till. Not all techniques are suitable for all land, but in most cases choosing the right techniques can substantially reduce soil loss.

An obvious queston then is why, after 50 years of soil conservation programs, are there still soil erosion problems of this magnitude if such erosion reduces yields as well as water and air quality and if technological solutions are available? Why are not the farmers of highly eroding acres practicing effective soil conservation?

The Traditional Analysis

Throughout the 50 years the United States has had soil conservation programs, farmers have held implicit user rights to the property they owned. Over the years, this allocation of rights to farmers has had widespread public support. The traditional view saw the farmer as a manager of nature, extracting a bounty to support the continued material prosperity for the nation. Private and unencumbered property rights were viewed by the general public and most economists as an efficient and appropriate means of securing that prosperity.

The property rights held by farmers implicitly entitled them to let their land erode if they so chose. Any changes in these rights had to be by mutual consent of all parties. An example of this can be found in the 1937 Standard Soil Conservation District Model Law. That law sponsored creation of local governmental units—soil conservation districts—with the potential exercise of considerable authority over land use planning. While all states ultimately adopted the standard act in various forms, none elected to implement strict land use regulation. Thus, almost all U.S. conservation policies have been voluntary, and most include cost-sharing with farmers. Cost-sharing is the setting of an acceptable price to change certain farming practices. The assumption was that such changes would reduce erosion.

Given this view of property rights, then, one can examine how much conservation was achieved by such programs and analyze how to achieve more conservation. Most economic and sociological research concerning farmers' conservation behavior has adopted this context. Such a context is appropriate when society's rules are not under serious debate and when improving the efficiency of a given system is considered desirable.

The traditional analysis of soil conservation views farmers as having the property right to allow the land to erode, views the farmer as a profit maximizer, and views conservation as an input to the production process. With this view, the farmer is seen as allocating his operating budget among various inputs—fertilizer, seed, herbicides, diesel fuel, and conservation practices—until the return to each input is equal. This assures the highest profits possible, given the size of the farmer's operating budget.

When conservation is viewed as an input to production, most analyses have found that conservation is not profitable (*19, 25, 26*). The reason usually cited is that most benefits from conservation occur in the future while most of the costs of conservation are in the present. At any reasonable rate of discount for the value of time, the future benefits of conservation are practically worthless in present dollars. With the traditional view, unless some markets were imperfect, farmers are making socially correct "decisions" by allowing soil erosion. There is no need for conservation policy if farmers have correctly calculated returns to conservation.

In explaining the existence of soil erosion or the need for conservation policy, therefore, the traditional analysis focuses on the variables that influence the costs and benefits of soil conservation and whether these costs and benefits are adequately assessed by the individual farmer and/or the land market. For example, there remains the possibility that farmers do not take discounted benefits into account, or that they do so incorrectly. They might be unaware of the on-farm damages caused by soil erosion, or they may incorrectly predict the rate at which land-saving technologies will emerge in the future.

This failure to discount correctly is not a problem if other farmers make the calculations correctly and the price of farmland accurately reflects its value in future production. If this is the case and the farmer of the eroding farm knows the various land values associated with eroding farmland, he or she will presumably adjust his or her farming practices until the value of the lost soil, as measured in increased farmland prices, equals the cost of saving it.

There has been some research on whether the market for farmland accurately reflects the future impacts of soil erosion. This research suggests that the market does indeed reflect some future impacts. But because information on the relationship of crop yields to soil erosion rates is not well known among farmers, or for that matter among soil scientists, the market does not fully reflect these relationships (*13*). If farmers lack knowledge about future yields, if they do not believe that erosion will affect future yields, if they predict future demand for crops will not lead to substantially increased prices, or if they believe land-saving technologies will be available to compensate for any erosion-caused reduction in yields, and if they are wrong, then the market value of land will not reflect the true cost of soil erosion to the farmer.

If the operator is a tenant on the land, then the value of the farmland is presumably not of concern to that individual. Furthermore, if the farmer cannot capture the future gains that arise from conservation decisions, he or she will have no incentive to conserve. It is not surprising that Ervin (*11*) found that rented land in Missouri had higher erosion rates than owned land despite having a slightly lower erosion potential than owned land. Hoover and Wiitala (*16*) found discrepencies between landlord and tenant preceptions of the soil erosion problem. Baron (*1*) found that farm owners who rented their land had lower conservation investment levels than those owners who also operated their lands.

The concern with benefits and costs leads to research into the adequacy of farmers' perceptions of their erosion problems as well. For example, several studies have found that perception of an erosion problem is requisite to the adoption of conservation practices (*9, 10, 17*). There also is research suggesting that farmers are more likely to recognize their neighbors' erosion problems than they do their own (*12, 16*).

This view of conservation behavior also leads researchers to investigate the possibility of capital constraints or time constraints that might inhibit the farmer from acting on his or her calculus of conservation's net benefits. Studies have examined the influence of a farmer's off-farm income, the net income of the farm, and the size of the farm. For example, several studies have investigated the influence of off-farm income on farmers' conservation behavior (*10, 16, 27*). Most found little relationship, but Forster and Stem (*14*) did find that operators who declared farming as their primary occupation also used more conservation practices on their farms. Some researchers have also found positive relationships between gross farm income and conservation adoption. Carlson, Dillman, and Lassey (*7*) found this to be the case for farmers in the Palouse area of Idaho. Other studies have not found such a positive relationship (*10, 22*). In contrast, several studies have found that large farm size tends to be positively associated with the adoption of conservation practices (*1, 7, 14, 16, 17, 18*).

Addressing both the calculus of conservation's costs and benefits to the individual farmer and the researching of capital constraints to investing in conservation also can include studies of such macro-economic variables as real interest rates, investment tax credits, or expected future prices due to monetary and fiscal policy impacts.

Policy Implications of the Traditional Analysis

Policy implications of the traditional analysis are fairly predictable. Because farmers have the property right to allow their land to erode, because they are profit maximizers, because most conservation practices are unprofitable, programs need to be devised to raise the benefits of conservation and/or lower the costs. This means that programs should include cost-sharing as well as technical assistance. Additional innovations focus on the need to reduce farmers' debt load with low interest loans or better use of the future markets. Furthermore, this traditional view leads to policy recommendations for educational programs that emphasize the need to improve farmers' perceptions of the erosion problem so that the perceptions more nearly represent those of soil conservation experts.

The narrow vision of traditional analysis has been subjected to considerable criticism, particularly by sociologists. They point out that farmers have numerous goals other than profit maximization—independence, maintaining a certain type and quality of life, maintaining social standing in their community, or meeting challenges. They also note that the rate of diffusion of knowledge concerning conservation practices goes through several stages of awareness, evaluation, trial, and adoption. This rate of diffusion also relates to the community characteristics, such as available support from conservation organizations, formal communication channels for disseminating information, and the informal communication networks among farmers (21).

Because of sociological insights, many traditional models are expanded to include various characteristics of farmers that might account for adoption behavior not accounted for by profit maximization. These characteristics include the amount of farmer contact with conservation organizations, the education level of the farmer, the age of the farmer, the race of the farmer, or the farmer's attitude toward risk. Nowak and Korching (22), for example, found that the number of contacts between a farm operator and various farm agency personnel were significantly and positively related to the number of conservation practices used by farmers in an Iowa watershed. However, Ervin and Ervin (10) found that the existence of a Soil Conservation Service conservation plan was not related to adoption of conservation practices. Several researchers have found that a farmer's age relates inversely to adoption of conservation practices (1, 11, 14). But Hoover and Wiitala (16) found that younger farmers, while more likely to recognize a soil erosion problem, were less likely to cooperate in a conservation program.

Similarly, several researchers have found that a higher level of education is a characteristic more likely associated with farmers who adopt conservation practices. Ervin and Ervin (10) and Nowak and Korsching (22) found that farmers tend not to use conservation practices if they are highly risk adverse. Neither the Ervin and Ervin study (10) nor the Norris study (20) found a relationship between expected transfer of the farm to a child and soil conservation. Also, Norris found that race did not significantly influence the adoption of soil conservation practices.

The policy implications of the expanded traditional model are considerably richer than the simple model. But effectively incorporating the sociological insights into programs is difficult. Once it is recognized that not all farmers will receive the information made available by agencies and that not all will react the same way, policy recommendations expand from those of the less sophisticated traditional model. The policy implications of the sociological contributions include selecting certain farmers for outreach programs, providing demonstration practices on the farms of recognized community leaders, placing more emphasis on the diffusion of knowledge, providing detailed technical assistance that allows the farmer to learn the appropriate technical skills, and providing for follow-up assistance in conservation programs.

An Alternative Perspective

The traditional view of property rights is less useful when property right assignments undergo change to achieve institutional redesign. This appears to be what is happening today. Increasingly, the public is challenging the traditional support of agriculture. The farmer is no longer perceived as a steward of the environment. The new vision of farming is more akin to an industrial production process and of the farmer as a corporate business person. The result has been increased control over farmers' use of water and wildlife habitat. In addition, soil conservation programs are undergoing increasing scrutiny.

As old property rights arrangements are challenged, the involved government focuses on such issues as the fair distribution of resources between users, regions, and time periods; the development of the appropriate values for society; and the determination of legitimate roles of government in distributing resources and shaping society values. Traditional analyses by economists and sociologists, while not useless, is less useful in this context. This is true in part because the factors of concern in a changing policy environment are precisely the ones usually held constant in the more traditional analysis. What is needed is a different type of analysis that focuses on the policy questions of changing property rights and the implications that flow therefrom.

There is an alternative perspective that focuses on the property rights structure but that finds the fee simple, absolute ownership assumption inappropriate. Where traditional analysis and policy design proceed with an idea of minimizing adverse affects on farmers and maintaining existing institutions, the alternative perspective does not take a protective stance toward the status quo. Indeed, the critical questions are the reverse of the traditional view. In the traditional view, agricultural analysis and, hence, policies are designed by asking what impacts resource quality, quantity, and price have on farmers' income and production. The alternative perspective asks the reverse—what impacts do current policies and farmers' practices have on resource quality and quantity. Thus, while traditional analysts calculate the impact of soil erosion on farmers' income or farmland values, analysts of the alternative perspective examine the impact of current institutions on farmers' practices. This perspective rejects the idea of finding an optimal policy design or an optimal level of soil erosion. It is instead concerned with the issues important to political decision-making. These issues are the design of institutions, the evolution and distribution of property rights, and the role of government in reflecting emerging values of society. In short, this perspective addresses issues that the traditional perspective normally ignores—values and equity.

Bromley (5), for example, suggests that three fundamental questions be posed with respect to resource allocations:

► Who is in control of management and rules (institutions) that determine the rate of use of natural resources?

► Who is in position to receive benefits arising from a particular use pattern?

► Who is exposed to the costs arising from the use of resources?

With soil erosion, the gainers appear to be current farmers. The losers are the next generation and current and future users of the various services of clean surface water and groundwater.

In this case, why soil erosion continues is explained by the separation of losses and gains. Farmers whose soil erosion problem has severe impacts on water quality may have little incentive, beyond an ethical one, to alleviate the problem. This is particularly true if the farmer perceives little damage to his or her farm's soil.

Yet in the past the United States has relied on voluntary programs and 50 percent cost-sharing to provide the needed incentive for conservation. Harrington, Krupnick, and Peskin (15) note that those nonconservation, voluntary programs that have been successful in the past share common elements. "The first condition is agreement that the policy objective is a worthy one and that the action sought will advance that objective. The second is easily observable noncompliance in order to create social pressures for compliance. The third is that the cost of a voluntary approach should not greatly exceed the value of its private benefits. The fourth is a belief that failure of the approach will eventually lead to mandatory government action." They conclude that, given these criteria, it is unlikely that a voluntary policy will effectively reduce soil erosion, particularly erosion that mainly causes water quality problems.

The alternative perspective that focuses on the distribution of benefits and costs and institutional incentives can lead the researcher to analyze a change in liability rules so that farmers bear responsibility for damages caused by erosion from their farms. For example, Ken Cook notes the disappointing progress the nation has made in reducing nonpoint pollution from agricultural sources (8). He states, "...we need to take a closer look at agriculture. Despite the continued dominance of family run operations, it is increasingly difficult to think of agriculture as a 'way of life'

that deserves to be held above the standards society demands of business-
es. And today's agriculture is undeniabley a business.... If we are honest,
we must admit that the voluntary approach has not so far done the job.
If we're realistic we must recognize that we'll probably never have a cost-
share program big enough to treat more than a small percentage of the
nonpoint problems...." These changes in liability may or may not be accompanied by compensation for the changing of farmers' historic property rights.

Not only does this suggest policy research on the design and impact of
regulations, it also illustrates analytic and policy concern with the "fair"
distribution of resources between time periods and between users.

The alternative perspective also questions the appropriateness of discounting future benefits as an equity question involving the distribution
of resources between generations. This questioning usually takes one of
two approaches, the "insurance" and the "ethical" approaches (2).

The insurance approach is based on the belief that "the majority may
consider that some resources for future eventualities should be maintained even when there is no apparent long-time economic justification...
for such conservation. Conservation in this case may be looked upon as a
form of insurance against technical changes which may or may not take
place" (6). In short, society should be willing to devote more resources to
insuring the maintenance of soil productivity than the farmer is willing to
devote to protecting against the "worse case" of high food and fiber
costs resulting from soil degradation. Thus, the insurance view is that a
society should be willing to act to retain the option for future soil use.

The ethical approach seriously questions whether the present generation has the right to discount the benefits to be received by future generations. This is the view represented by Pigou (24): "There is wide agreement that the state should protect the interests of the future in some degree against the effects of our irrational discounting, and of our preference for ourselves over our descedents. The whole movement for 'conservation' in the United States is based upon this conviction. It is the clear
duty of government which is the trustee for unborn generations as well as
for its present citizens, to watch over and if need be, by legislative enact-
ment, to defend exhaustible natural resources of the country from rash
and reckless spoilation."

With the ethical approach, soil conservation becomes a moral issue.
Soil should be husbanded and given to the next generation in a condition
that provides for that generation's welfare.

Both the insurance approach and the ethical approach can be interpreted as rationales for society's obligation to protect soil's protectivity,
as well as air and water quality, at least to a safe minimum standard—
whenever the costs of doing so are not unreasonably large (2).

The alternative perspective explains why soil erosion continues by noting the disparity between the costs and benefits between users (as in the case of water quality) as well as between generations (as in the case of discounting). Part of the discounting argument is that unacceptably high rates of soil erosion continue because of differing acceptable levels of risk taking for individuals than for society as a whole.

If existing property rights are viewed as subject to change, the policies that eminate from such analysis focus on regulation and institutional design (including the improvement of existing institutions and markets). If existing property rights are viewed as subject to change through the eminent domain powers of the state, then the policies that eminate from such analysis include compensation. For example, through conservation reserves or conservation easements farmers might agree to abide by certain conservation standards (planting marginal land to trees) with compensation (payment of a lease fee). Other analyses might address how such compensation revenue could be obtained. One example might be fees on downstream users of water, such as commercial fishermen, to generate revenues that could be used to compensate upstream users of the watershed, farmers.

The alternative perspective also promotes the questioning of past programs' influences on soil erosion. While the nation has had more than a half century of agricultural and conservation programs, the impact of these programs on soil use and water quality has only recently been examined.

Farm programs have attempted to improve farm income through demand expansion (export programs), supply control (acreage restriction programs), price and income supports, or subsidized inputs (low-cost loans). Tracing the impacts of these programs on soil and water quality is exceptionally difficult. What few studies are available are not conclusive as to the impact of these programs on conservation in the aggregate. In some cases, such as disaster programs, these programs have exacerbated soil erosion problems. The predominant objective of agricultural programs has been to raise and stabilize farm income. Conservation impact has not been particularly relevant to this goal. Thus, natural resource impacts, both positive and negative, were basiclly unintended and largely ignored (3).

A similar statement can be made about traditional soil conservation programs. A review of the motivation for and use of these conservation programs indicates the programs were used mainly to improve farmers' incomes. As a result, these programs have been less effective in conserving soil than they could have been had conservation been the predominant policy goal (3). Studies have shown, for example, that only 21 percent of the federally cost-shared conservation practices were placed on land eroding at greater than 14 tons per acre per year. More than half the cost-shared conservation practices were applied on cropland experiencing less than 5 tons per acre per year of sheet and rill erosion (*29*).

The conclusions from studies of this type have led to policy implications that include cross-compliance and targeting. Cross-compliance makes the receipt of agricultural program benefits contingent on farmers' practicing soil conservation. Sodbuster provisions, which deny federal price supports, crop insurance, and other program benefits to farmers who plow highly erodible land, are one example of cross-compliance.

Targeting involves the selection of specific regions or farms to receive special assistance to reduce soil erosion problems. This perspective leads policy analysts to carefully examine the criteria by which the selection of targeted areas is made. Targeting on the basis of high erosion rates might miss many regions with water quality problems. Indeed, targeting to high erosion rates does not necessarily assure adequate attention to soil productivity either. Some highly erodible land also may include very deep fertile soils and thus not suffer a soil productivity decline with high erosion. On the other hand, land with low quality subsoils near the surface, but with low erosion rates, might be in need of even more protection if soil fertility is to be maintained.

These analyses and policy implications stem from the focus of the alternative perspective on the role of government in reflecting society's values. This is particularly evident with respect to cross-compliance. Several studies have suggested that cross-compliance, at least as usually discussed, will not prove to be an effective method of reducing soil erosion (*3, 23*). It is, however, an attractive strategy on the basis of fairness and ethical behavior.

A Matter of Appropriateness

The question of why soil erosion continues is clearly a complex one. It cannot be adequately answered by a narrow, traditional approach that assumes conservation is only another agricultural input in the pursuit of profits. While sociologists and anthropologists can provide additional realism and richness to the traditional model, it is necessary to consider the role of property rights and other institutions as well as society's values to achieve a good understanding of why soil erosion continues.

Once that understanding is obtained, however, it does not in itself answer what should be the nation's policy toward soil erosion. This requires consideration of ethics, values, and equity. The alternative perspective to the more traditional analysis has considerable usefulness in addressing the policy questions of interest. While all the research discussed above can assist in developing policy recommendations and while there is considerably more research that could be undertaken, the type of analysis that comes from the alternative perspective appears to be the most approriate in a period when the American public appears to be undergoing a profound change of beliefs with respect to the farmers' use of natural resources.

REFERENCES

1. Baron, Donald. 1981. *Landownership characteristics and investment in soil conservation.* Staff Report No. AGES810911. Economic Research Service, U.S. Department of Agriculture, Washington, D.C.
2. Batie, Sandra S. 1983. *Soil erosion: Crisis in America's croplands?* The Conservation Foundation, Washington, D.C.
3. Batie, Sandra S. 1984. *Agricultural policy and soil conservation: Implications for the 1985 Farm Bill.* American Enterprise Institute, Washington, D.C.
4. Batie, Sandra S., Leonard A. Shabman, and Randall A. Kramer. 1985. *U.S. agriculture and natural resource policy: Past and future.* In C. Ford Runge (editor) *The Future of the North American Granary: Politics, Economics, and Resource Constraints in American Agriculture.* Iowa State University Press, Ames.
5. Bromley, Daniel W. 1982. *Land and water problems: An institutional perspective.* American Journal of Agricultural Economics 64: 834-844.
6. Bunce, A. C. 1945. *Economics of soil conservation.* Iowa State College Press, Ames.
7. Carlson, John E., Don A. Dillman, and William R. Lassey. 1981. *The farmer and erosion: Factors influencing the use of control practices.* Bulletin No. 601. Idaho Agricultural Experiment Station, Moscow.
8. Cook, Ken. 1985. *Agricultural pollution control: A time for sticks?* Journal of Soil and Water Conservation 40(11): 105-106.
9. Earle, T. R., C. W. Rose, and A. A. Brownlea. 1979. *Socioeconomic predictors of intention towards soil conservation and their implication in environmental management.* Journal of Environmental Management (9): 225-236.
10. Ervin, Christine A., and David E. Ervin. 1982. *Factors affecting the use of soil conservation practices: Hypotheses, evidence and policy implications.* Land Economics 58(3): 277-292.
11. Ervin, David E. 1981. *Soil erosion on owned and rented cropland: Economic models and evidence.* Department of Agricultural Economics, University of Missouri, Columbia.
12. Ervin, David E., and Charles T. Alexander. 1981. *Soil erosion and conservation in Monroe Co., Missouri: Farmers' perceptions, attitudes and performances.* Department of Agricultural Economics, University of Missouri, Columbia.
13. Ervin, David E., and John W. Mill. 1985. *Agricultural land markets and soil erosion: Policy relevance and conceptual issues.* American Journal of Agricultural Economics (in press).
14. Forster, D. Lynn, and George L. Stem. 1979. *Adoption of reduced tillage and other conservation practices in the Lake Erie Basin.* U.S. Army Corps of Engineers, Buffalo, New York.
15. Harrington, Winston, Alan J. Krupnick, and Henry M. Peskin. 1985. *Policies for nonpoint source water pollution control.* Journal of Soil and Water Conservation 40(1): 27-32.
16. Hoover, Herbert, and Marc Wiitala. 1980. *Operator and landlord participation in soil erosion control in the Maple Creek watershed in northeast Nebraska.* Staff Report NRED 80-4. Economics, Statistics, and Cooperatives Service, U.S. Department of Agriculture, Washington, D.C.
17. Lasley, Paul, and Michael Nolan. 1981. *Landowner attitudes toward soil and water conservation in the Grindstone-Lost Muddy Creek project.* Department of Rural Sociology, University of Missouri, Columbia.
18. Miranowski, John A. 1982. *Overlooked variables in BMP implementation: Risk attitudes, perceptions, and human capital characteristics.* In Lee A. Christensen and John A. Miranowski [editors] *Perceptions, Attitudes and Risk: Overlooked Variables in Formulating Public Policy on Soil Conservation and Water Quality.* Economic Research Service, U.S. Department of Agriculture, Washington, D.C.
19. Mitchell, J. K., J. C. Brach, and E. R. Swanson. 1980. *Costs and benefits of terraces*

      for erosion control. Journal of Soil and Water Conservation 35(5): 233-236.
20. Norris, Patricia E. 1985. *Factors influencing the adoption of soil conservation practice in Virginia's Piedmont Bright Leaf Erosion Control Area.* M.S. thesis. Department of Agricultural Economics, Virginia Polytechnic Institute and State University, Blacksburg.
21. Nowak, Peter J., and Peter F. Korsching. 1985. *Conservation tillage: Revolution or evolution?* Journal of Soil and Water Conservation 40(2): 199-201.
22. Nowak, Peter J., and Peter F. Korsching. 1982. *Social and institutional factors affecting the adoption and maintenance of agricultural BMPs.* In F. Schaller and G. Bailey [editors] *Agricultural Management and Water Quality.* Iowa State University Press, Ames, Iowa.
23. Ogg, Clayton W., and James A. Zellner. 1984. *A conservation reserve: Conserving soil and dollars.* Journal of Soil and Water Conservation 39(2): 92-94.
24. Pigou, A. C. 1924. *The economics of welfare.* Macmillan and Co., Ltd., London, England.
25. Rosenberry, P., R. Knutson, and L. Harman. 1980. *Predicting the effects of soil depletion from erosion.* Journal of Soil and Water Conservation 35(5): 131-134.
26. Seitz, W. D., C. R. Taylor, R.G.F. Spitze, C. Osteen, and M. C. Nelson. 1979. *Economic impacts of soil erosion.* Land Economics 55(1): 28-42.
27. Taylor, David L., and William L. Miller. 1978. *The adoption process and environmental innovations: A case study of a government project.* Rural Sociology 43: 634-648.
28. U.S. Department of Agriculture. 1982. *A national program for soil and water conservation.* Final Report and Environmental Impact Statement, Soil and Water Resources Conservation Act 1977, Washington, D.C.
29. U.S. Department of Agriculture, Agricultural Stabilization and Conservation Service. 1981. *National summary, evaluation of the agricultural conservation program: Phase I.* Washington, D.C.

2

Macro-economics of Soil Conservation

John A. Miranowski

Many of us grew up with the belief that "as goes the agricultural economy so goes the national economy." This popular misconception of causality probably arose as a result of the agricultural distress of the 1920s, followed by the general depression of the 1930s. Also, economic activity in the agricultural sector was a much larger proportion of total economic activity in the earlier stages of our nation's economic development.

Only in the last decade or so have we come to recognize fully the profound impacts that macro-economic variables have on the agricultural economy. Edward Schuh's classic article "The New Macroeconomics of Agriculture" succeeded in stimulating research on the role of macro-economic factors in determining the fate of agricultural activity (8). Many traditional theories explaining agricultural cycles are now being recast in terms of macro-economics forces (2).

What do these reconsiderations of macro-economics have to do with soil conservation investments and activities or, more generally, with land purchases and improvements? Many key variables influencing soil conservation actions are beyond the control of agricultural and conservation policy. Moreover, to achieve a long-run soil conservation objective may require the selection of conservation programs less sensitive to macro--economic forces.

Setting the Conservation Stage

The traditional economic argument for governmental intervention in resource allocation is this: the market fails to provide for an efficient

15

allocation of resources over time; governmental intervention can improve the allocation.

Is there evidence that the farmland market fails to protect long-run soil productivity? Although it has long been hypothesized that such is the case, recent research does not support this hypothesis (4, 6). Given evidence from the Iowa farmland market, land purchasers are not ignorant of soil erosion's impacts on productivity and expected net returns. Both topsoil depth and soil erodibility are significant in explaining county- and farm-level differences in land values.

Although such results indicate the land market works, they fail to indicate how well the market functions. Taking the analysis a step further and relating an estimate of the value of the marginal product of soil depth and erodibility to the implicit prices paid for these soil characteristics led to the conclusion that the market functions quite effectively (4).[1] Such results do require a few qualifications. First, the analysis was only applied to one state using county-level data. Similar experiments need to be replicated in other areas and at more disaggregated levels (6). Second, in deriving the value of the marginal product, representative market prices were used. If these prices do not reflect land purchasers' expectations and/or long-run market prices, then the results may be misleading. Third, substantial uncertainties about future world food demands, production technologies, and resource productivity exist and may or may not be included in the value of the land. Under these circumstances, it is likely that society may choose to invest in additional soil conservation above and beyond the dictates of the market to ensure adequate soil productivity in the future. Fourth, the environmental (off-farm) impacts of soil erosion are ignored by the market process. Impacts that are external to landowner decisions cannot be captured in the land market. Moreover, off-site impacts are not necessarily correlated with the productivity impacts, so there is no assurance that these impacts will be indirectly considered. Government intervention is required to protect society's interest in environmental quality.

It is also important to recognize that soil conservation problems are long run in nature (5). Changing short-run phenomena—credit constraints, interest rates, commodity prices—are not signs of market failure and as such do not require governmental intervention. With the exception of isolated situations, soil productivity is not lost in a short time period (1). Also, the market reacts to new and improved information as soil productivity gradually changes. As a result, errors in terms of too much or too little soil conservation are continually being corrected. More serious soil allocation distortions may be introduced by commodity,

---

[1]Evidence from the EPIC and PI models tends to support the productivity impact estimates in this analysis.

credit, tax, and water development programs. These programs distort relative input and output prices and, hence, soil conservation activities over time.

Land Investment and Macro-economic Factors

Macro-economic and international policies are not developed with any thought about their impacts on soil conservation decisions. Nor can a convincing argument be made that they should. But it is important to recognize the impact of macro-economic forces on investment in and adoption of soil conservation practices. Although it is simplistic to think of conservation investment in the same context as farmland investment, the analysis can be presented in that framework because the decisions are similar and designed to acquire or maintain productive capacity. It is assumed in the analysis that a landowner's objective is to maximize the present value of future economic rents, which may include investments to maintain productivity.

A simple land investment model is used. Although not a rigorous treatment of the investment decision, the model serves to illustrate the influence of changing parameters (including macro-economic and international factors) on the expected net returns to land and land improvements (including soil conservation practices).

Two assumptions used in the analysis are important. First, individuals presumably are indifferent to land purchases versus land improvements when the net present value of both alternatives is the same. Second, it is assumed that macro-economic factors can be treated as exogeneous variables in the model because agricultural factors will have no significant influence on the general economy. These assumptions may be a subject for lively debate, but they are made for ease of presentation.

The value of land or land improvement for agricultural production purposes is a function of the present value of expected net returns from that land or land improvement. The same economic valuation applies to the purchase of any capital asset or improvement.

The value of any land parcel or improvement is

$$V = \sum_{t=1}^{n} \frac{NR_t}{(1+r-i)^t} \qquad [1]$$

where V is the value of parcel or improvement, NR_t is the expected net return from production in year t, r is the expected long-run borrowing (interest) rate, and i is the anticipated rate of inflation. If the cost of the capital asset (land price) or improvement (conservation practice) is less than or equal to the present value of the expected return, then invest. If not, the discounted expected return will not cover the capital cost. Alternatively, if $V - C \geq 0$, then invest; or if $V - C < 0$, then take no action, where C is the cost of the capital asset or improvement.

In reality, the actual capital investment decision may be more complex and uncertain. This is especially so given the macro-economic factors that will influence the expected outcome. Stability does not characterize the recent historic pattern of macro-economic variables.

In any investment decision, discounted future (expected) net returns are weighed against investment costs, C, that occur primarily in the current period. Uncertainty over future net returns, interest rates and inflation may result in suboptimal soil conservation investments and the need for governmental intervention (3). Yet the same uncertainty enters into all agricultural investment decisions, and to some extent all private investment decisions, requiring more general monetary and fiscal solutions as opposed to singling out conservation investments. Also, equation 1 assumes perfect foresight with respect to the future values of variables and ignores the whole expectations-formation process.

What are the macro-economic factors that drive conservation investment decisions? Inflation reduces the real cost of borrowing. Low and sometimes negative real interest rates in the 1970s should have stimulated both land improvements and conservation investments. The current 7 to 8 percent real rate of interest reduces the incentive to invest, especially in soil conservation, which typically has a long benefit stream.

Exchange rates will have a major impact on expected returns to conservation investments. A strong U.S. dollar in world financial markets reduces international demand for U.S. farm commodities, lowers commodity prices, reduces expected returns in the numerator of equation 1, and discourages soil conservation investments. Budget deficits may also deter conservation investments by creating upward pressure on interest rates and stimulating capital inflows that may strengthen the U.S. dollar and thereby reduce demand for U.S. farm products.[2]

Tax policies may also have major impact on conservation investments. Current tax policies provide incentives to stimualate capital investment. The proposed tax reform initiative would have even more profound impacts. For example, lower tax rates will increase return on investment, at least in the short run. But denying current deductions for capital (conservation) expenditures will expand the income tax base, increase tax liability, and reduce conservation investments.

Some Empirical Evidence

Given the current paucity of time series data on private soil conservation investment, it is not possible to develop and estimate an econometric

---

[2]At the same time, reduced international demand may reduce total cropland acreage and the need for conservation investments.

investment model. But efforts are underway to develop improved data series on land improvement investments so that such analyses can be conducted in the future.

Data on private investment in soil conservation practices are not available on an annual basis over time.[3] However, annual data series are available for land improvements (1975-1984, irrigation (1971-1984), and total land and farm improvements (1971-1984) from the Farm Produc-

[3]A periodic time series on natural resource capital has been developed by George Pavelis, but is not available on an annual basis (7).

Table 1. Private conservation and farm improvement investments 1971-1984. *

Year	Land Improvements	Irrigation Improvements	Total Land and Improvements
		\$/millions	
1971	317	237	897
1972	na	480	989
1973	na	557	1,229
1974	na	781	1,586
1975	517	934	1,857
1976	634	740	2,001
1977	600	840	2,092
1978	581	540	1,729
1979	643	635	1,029
1980	717	621	2,103
1981	1,170	529	2,490
1982	625	460	1,806
1983	779	318	1,694
1984	613	359	1,449
		1972 \$/millions	
1971	335	251	948
1972	na	480	989
1973	na	523	1,153
1974	na	609	1,237
1975	386	675	1,342
1976	455	532	1,438
1977	407	569	1,417
1978	357	331	1,061
1979	346	342	1,091
1980	342	296	1,002
1981	529	239	1,126
1982	275	202	794
1983	333	136	725
1984	251	147	593

*Farm Production Economics Survey.

tion Expenditures Survey conducted by the Economic Research Service. The land improvements category includes dams and ponds, terraces, drainage ditches and tile lines, land clearing and leveling, and other soil conservation facilities. Although soil conservation cannot be separated from drainage activities, the aggregate does represent investments under-

Table 2. Factors influencing conservation and capital improvement activities, 1971-1984.

Year	Trade-Weighted Value of U.S. Dollar	Prices Received for Crops Index	Prices Paid for Production Inputs Index	Crop Productivity per Acre Index
1971	118	56	57	96
1972	109	60	61	99
1973	99	91	73	99
1974	101	117	83	88
1975	98	105	91	96
1976	106	102	97	94
1977	103	100	100	100
1978	92	105	108	105
1979	88	116	125	113
1980	87	125	138	99
1981	103	134	148	113
1982	117	121	150	116
1983	125	127	153	99
1984	138	139	155	112

Year	Federal Land Bank Bank New Loan Rate (%)	Production Credit Association Average Cost of Loans (%)	Agricultural Land Values Index	Change in Implicit GNP Deflator (%)
1971	7.9	7.3	43	4.7
1972	7.4	7.0	47	3.2
1973	7.5	8.1	53	5.6
1974	8.1	9.4	66	9.7
1975	8.7	8.9	75	9.3
1976	8.7	8.2	86	5.2
1977	8.4	7.9	100	6.0
1978	8.4	8.8	109	7.3
1979	9.2	10.7	125	8.5
1980	10.4	12.9	145	9.0
1981	11.3	14.9	158	9.4
1982	12.3	14.3	157	6.0
1983	11.6	11.5	148	3.8
1984	na	na	146	

Sources: Agricultural Statistics - 1984, Economic Report of the President, February, 1985.

taken to maintain and increase the supply of productive cropland. Presumably, farm operators and owners will allocate their investments between cropland supply-enhancing and expanding investments based on the relative private returns to each alternative. Thus, the aggregate land improvement category should more accurately reflect investment behavior in response to expected net farm returns and real interest rates.

Considering real investment levels in table 1, the peak levels were achieved in the 1974-1977 period for all three investment categories as well as in 1981 for the land improvement category. Are these investment peaks consistent with the values for the right-hand side variables that would enter or influence equation 1?

First, net returns, NR_t, were high in the mid-1970s. The most favorable spread between prices received and prices paid by farmers was in the 1973-1976 period (Table 2), even though this spread was somewhat offset by productivity growth in the 1980s. These results are partially a function of the strength (value) of the U.S. dollar in international markets. The U.S. dollar was weak in the 1973-1975 and 1978-1980 periods. It gained strength again in the 1980s.

Second, real interest rates (nominal rates less inflation as represented by the gross national product deflator) were low in the 1970s and negative for longer term investments in 1974-1975, again coinciding with the peak of investment activity. When real interest rates increased dramatically in the 1980s, soil and water investments declined significantly. Because investors base their capital improvement decisions on long-term capital costs, it is necessary to take investors long-term expectations into account and not place too much emphasis on current rates. But the relationship must be taken as more than coincidental.

Third, to the extent that cash flow and debt burden influence soil and water conservation investment decisions, nominal net cash flow was highest in 1973 and the 1978-1981 period, and nominal real estate debt (which could encompass many conservation investments) was increasing significantly in the 1980s (Table 3). Cash flow apparently was not highly correlated with investment, but an increasing debt load may have placed further constraints on conservation investment.

Fourth, the current definition of conservation investment ignores farmers' efforts to shift to conservation tillage as a means of reducing soil and water losses. Table 4 provides a summary of minimum till and no-till activities over the 1973-1984 period. Unfortunately, a change in the data source after 1982 limits the comparisons that can be made. If the data series were consistent over time, it is highly likely that minimum tillage would have demonstrated a consistent increase over time. There does not appear to have been a response comparable to the land improvement investments. But conservation tillage is a production practice that is largely being adopted in response to improved short-run profitability.

For instance, rapidly increasing production costs are outpacing commodity price increases (Table 2). To maintain net returns, farmers are adopting conservation tillage. The no-till index decline in 1979-1981 is probably explained by declining real energy prices following the energy crises of the 1970s.

Finally, the land values index in table 2 was less sensitive to macroeconomic forces than capital improvements (including conservation investments). Although beyond the scope of this paper to develop an explanation, it does raise some important issues in modeling and interpreting land value adjustments. Contrary to the initial hypothesis that land investments and capital improvements could be accorded parallel treatment, the decision to purchase land is apparently different than the decision to improve existing land. In other words, the two alternatives may not be good substitutes.

Tax policy may also have a major impact on conservation investment, but data are not available to treat the issue explicitly. The current deductibility of conservation investment will reduce the cost, C, of the conservation practice. Yet the deduction will be more advantageous to farmers during profitable periods and to farmers showing a positive taxable income, regardless of conservation need. Other tax incentives may encourage sodbusting and swampbusting by both farmer and nonfarmer investors and aggravate the problems of soil erosion, groundwater mining, and

Table 3. Farm income and balance sheet, 1971-1984.

Year	Farm Real Estate Assets	Farm Real Estate Debt	Gross Farm Receipts	Net Farm Income	Net Cash Flow
	$/billions				
1971	223	30	22	15	18
1972	240	32	26	20	25
1973	267	35	41	34	40
1974	328	40	51	27	35
1975	360	45	46	26	30
1976	418	50	49	20	30
1977	496	55	49	20	31
1978	555	63	54	28	40
1979	655	71	63	32	48
1980	756	85	73	21	40
1981	828	96	73	31	40
1982	819	106	75	22	35
1983	769	110	70	16	34
1984	764	112	na	na	na

Sources: Agricultural Statistics - 1984. Economic Report of the President, February 1985.

Table 4. Conservation tillage levels, 1973-1984.

1973	62	67	2.0	15.8
1974	71	75	2.1	17.0
1975	77	89	2.4	17.6
1976	83	103	2.7	18.4
1977	100	100	2.5	21.0
1978	108	98	2.4	22.7
1979	114	92	2.5	23.9
1980	132	98	2.4	27.5
1981	141	119	2.9	29.1
1982	160	159	3.6	31.7
1983	127	161	3.9	26.8*
1984	136	203	4.5	25.8

Sources: *No-Till Farmer,* Conservation Tillage Information Center (CTIC).
*The 1983 decline in minimum till may be partially explained by the PIK Program and a shift from *No-Till Farmer* data to CTIC data.

wetlands drainage. Thus, on balance, current tax policies may be more detrimental to maintaining and enhancing long-run productivity than to protecting it.

Policy Implications

Although macroeconomic variables are beyond the control of soil conservation policy, these forces may have a major impact on soil conservation decisions. Some conservation programs may not accomplish the desired change in conservation activities because of the overriding importance of macroeconomic forces. For example, cost-sharing is designed to reduce the installation or adoption cost for particular conservation practices. Although the conservation subsidy, on average, will reduce the landowner's or operator's cost and increase the attractiveness of conservation investment, the timing leaves something to be desired.

The present value of the expected benefits (V in equation 1) is highly variable over time. When export demand is high and real interest rates are low (as during the boom of the 1970s), V is higher. This provides a greater incentive for private investment. In the mid-1980s, when demand for agricultural exports was weak, real interest rates were high, and V was low, there was little incentive to invest in soil conservation, even with cost-sharing available. Cost-sharing subsidies only induce conservation investment if private returns exceed private costs. To reduce private costs sufficiently may require unacceptably high cost-sharing levels in the 1980s. Generally, the macroeconomic impact can be expected to swamp the cost-sharing subsidies.

The effectiveness of education and technical assistance programs is also a function of the returns to conservation investment. These programs improve the information available to farmers and lower the cost of conservation. But they may be unable to counteract changes in the current value of expected benefits.

Although some individuals may argue for countercyclical conservation policy during periods of depressed financial conditions in agriculture—1930s and 1980s—the record with such efforts in the macro-economic arena does not provide strong support for the countercyclical approach. Moreover, if such a policy approach is appropriate for soil conservation, similar arguments should apply to other natural resources, such as oil.

The policy goal should be to achieve the socially desired level of conservation investment over time regardless of short-run economic fluctuations. Casual evidence suggests a cyclical response of conservation investment. Because soil conservation is a long-run issue, we must differentiate the long-run, socially optimal rate of investment from the short-run cyclical rates and pursue policies designed to achieve the long-run, socially optimal rate.

The ability of traditional conservation policy to achieve the socially optimal level of conservation investment is probably limited. Research that develops new conservation technologies and lowers the cost of conservation practices (e.g., improved conservation tillage alternatives) may be the best long-run conservation policy option. The conservation reserve provision in the 1985 farm bill, which provides for the long-term retirement of highly erodible land, provides a more stable and effective longer run solution. But future land retirement may prove costly during periods of improved demand if highly erodible land is to be maintained in grass or trees into the foreseeable future.

Periods such as the 1970s and 1980s reflect the market system at work, adjusting to expectations and responding to previous errors. These adjustments affect land values and conservation investments. Unfortunately, such market adjustments place heavy burdens on some individuals and may cause catastrophic financial situations for others. The public response to the plight of landowners and farmers is beyond the economic efficiency dimensions of conservation policy and is more appropriately addressed in the financial policy arena.

REFERENCES

1. Crosson, Pierre. 1983. *Productivity effects of cropland erosion in the United States.* Resources for the Future, Washington, D.C.
2. Enders, Walter, and Barry Falk. 1984. *A microeconomic test of money neutrality.* Review of Economics and Statistics 66: 666-669.
3. Kiker, Clyde F. 1985. *A financial perspective on soil erosion.* In Lee A. Christensen [editor] *Natural Resource Issues and Agricultural Policy: Ideas from a Symposium.* Staff Rpt. AGES850420. Economic Research Service, U.S. Department of Agriculture,

Washington, D.C.
4. Miranowski, John A. 1983. *An implicit price model of the impact of soil and locational characteristics on land prices.* Department of Economics, Iowa State University, Ames.
5. Miranowski, John A. 1984. *Impacts of productivity loss on crop production and management in a dynamic economic model.* American Journal of Agricultural Economics 66: 61-71.
6. Miranowski, John A., and Brian D. Hammes. 1984. *Implicit prices of soil characteristics for farmland in Iowa.* American Journal of Agricultural Economics 66: 745-749.
7. Pavelis, George A. 1985. *Natural resource capital formation in American agriculture: Irrigation, drainage, and conservation, 1855-1980.* Staff Report AGES850725. Economic Research Service, U.S. Department of Agriculture, Washington, D.C.
8. Schuh, G. Edward. 1976. *The new macroeconomics of agriculture.* American Journal of Agricultural Economics 58: 803-811.

3

Soil and Water Conservation: A Farm Structural and Public Policy Context

Frederick H. Buttel and Louis E. Swanson

Among the intriguing aspects of social science research are the instances in which the very social and economic phenomena we value and from which great wealth is generated also may be associated with undesirable consequences. Persistent soil and water degradation as a consequence of agriculture is one such example. Continued degradation of soil and water resources is a costly externality of the way in which we as a society produce food and fiber. Inherent characteristics of U.S. agriculture not only are associated with the degradation of these two vital natural resources, but these characteristics also are associated with the most recent crisis among America's family farms. Unfortunately, these two issues are not perceived as complementary. Consequently, issues centered around soil and water degradation have been given low policy priority.

Most national meetings on agricultural policy issues today are given over to discussing the farm bill and, most importantly, how agricultural policymakers will deal with the devastating farm financial crisis. In Washington, D.C., now, soil conservation among executive and congressional policymakers is a nonissue. Amid the specter of thousands of farmers threatened with insolvency, it is almost impossible to convince anyone that soil conservation deserves even as much as benign neglect. For example, the Soil Conservation Service is slated for substantial cuts in its already underfunded budget. In addition, there is little attempt to connect conceptually the current farm crisis with the underfunded threat to soil and water resources.

Mention of these sobering realities is not meant to downplay the current work in agricultural resource conservation. Indeed, agricultural resource conservation is a pressing policy concern. But soil and water conservation is clearly on the downside of the issue-attention curve, the peak for which occurred two or so years ago. Today, soil conservation fails to hold the attention of the policymaking and scholarly communities as well as the public at large.

In retrospect, many of the assumptions used in research and policy formulation a short while back now seem time-bound. Concern about soil erosion just a few years ago focussed on the potentially adverse impacts on U.S. productive capacity in a global economy with a seemingly insatiable demand for U.S. grains, oilseeds, and fibers. Clearly, this situation no longer holds. Hope for expanded federal cost-sharing in soil conservation was displaced by the massive assault on virtually all nonmilitary programs other than social security and some other politically sensitive entitlement programs because of the deepening federal fiscal crisis.

Has there been inadequate attention in social science research on soil and water conservation to macro-social or macro-economic levels of reasoning and inquiry? Definitely! While research at the micro level has been fruitful in advancing knowledge about farmers' conservation decisions, these approaches are incomplete, as is the case now that the incentives for adopting soil and water conservation have become decidedly adverse. Macro-structural reasoning and research are *not* superior to micro-social inquiry. But these two approaches are different, and each generates different types of knowledge.

Agricultural economics and rural sociology in the United States historically have shown a marked preference for micro approaches. Among the reasons for micro emphases has been the fact that research at this level appears more directly applicable to policy. Despite the seemingly greater applicability of micro approaches to policy development, however, it is important to combine micro and macro approaches in order to understand the changing configuration of the policy environment. Furthermore, overemphasis of micro approaches with respect to the continuing problems of soil erosion may hide important structural constraints to on-farm conservation decision-making. There are some general policy implications of a macro-structural perspective on soil and water conservation, a number of which contradict implications drawn from micro research. Resolution of these contradictory policy implications is a high priority for soil and water conservation policy research.

Agricultural Resource Degradation

Soil erosion and the transport of nutrients, pesticides, salts, and pathogens by surface and subsurface water occur, to varying degrees, on and under more than 2 million farms in the United States. Soil erosion and the transport of materials by water off a farm are natural processes. These processes are accelerated by certain tillage, cropping, and other cultural practices. The incidence of these problems varies geographically. Sheet and rill erosion are severe in portions of Washington, Idaho, and Oregon; the western Corn Belt; the uplands of the southern Mississippi Valley; and parts of Maine (2). Wind erosion mainly afflicts the southern Great Plains. Surface and subsurface transport of chemicals, especially fertilizers, pesticides, and salts, tends to occur where the use of land-saving inputs has intensified agricultural production.

Historically, agricultural resource degradation in the United States has been approached almost exclusively from two complementary perspectives. First, the problem has been conceptualized in terms of the long-term deterioration of land productivity. Second, solutions to the problems of soil erosion and runoff of chemicals have been viewed largely in terms of voluntary compliance by farmers. If farmers were the ultimate victims of the land-productivity-reducing effects of soil erosion and runoff, we should expect farmers to make a significant share of the investment required to protect agricultural land productivity. The agricultural resource management task thus becomes one of convincing farmers to adopt new technologies and cultural practices to reduce soil erosion and runoff. This is generally done on the basis that it is in the farm household's interest to do so. Improved resource management is sometimes thought of as a stewardship obligation of farmers also. But with cuts in an already underfunded budget, it is unreasonable to assume that SCS can convince farmers to participate voluntarily in cost-sharing programs when their scarce capital resources are more profitably applied to other areas of their production process.

Looking at soil erosion and related problems in terms of lost productivity and at solutions to these problems in terms of farmers' self-interest has a clear political root: the historical reluctance politically to subject financially strapped family farmers to regulatory measures. In part, this is because the federal government has been slow to undertake regulation in general (1, 18) and water quality regulation in particular (25). Landmark environmental legislation in the early 1970s, including the Federal Water Polluton Control Act Amendments, in effect exempted farmers from regulation. This de facto exemption of farmers from water quality regulation appears to have been due less to the exercise of political power by farmers than to the fact that family farming has long been a powerful political symbol. Regulation of farmers in a manner comparable to corporate polluters was clearly outside the range of political acceptability.

This event was but the latest in the longstanding legacy: agricultural resource conservation should be achieved through voluntary farmer compliance and the logic of the long-term economic interests of farmers, not through regulation. Accordingly, the predominant focus of SCS over its

50-year history has been to use modest levels of financial inducement, such as cost-sharing, to leverage farmer decision-making and, most recently, to encourage the voluntary use of tillage innovations, such as conservation tillage.

While debate continues about whether soil erosion and other forms of agricultural resource degradation have become worse over the past 20 years, it seems fair to say that progress has been modest at best. This demonstrates the limits of voluntary programs. Moreover, there is substantial evidence suggesting that an important dimension of agricultural resource degradation problems has been ignored. The key issue involved, many have maintained, is the loss of long-term soil productivity and a reduction in the productive capacity of U.S. agriculture. But the evidence suggests that soil erosion and runoff extract important off-site costs that increasingly have made soil conservation an ecological and political issue outside of farming.

As noted, soil erosion and runoff problems are unevenly distributed across space. About 60 percent of U.S. cropland exhibits combined soil losses from sheet, rill, and wind erosion that are less than 5 tons per acre annually. Annual soil losses exceed 25 tons per acre on only 8.6 percent of the nation's cropland, and 70 percent of all "excess" erosion—more than 5 tons per acre per year—occurs on this 8.6 percent of cropland (2). Moreover, a substantial proportion of this 8.6 percent of cropland is relatively marginal in terms of U.S. productive capacity because of steep slopes and other constraints. An additional proportion is capable of sustaining staggering soil erosion losses, 25 tons per acre per year or more, on a virtually indefinite basis with no significant loss of productive potential (20). The proportion of prime U.S. farmland that stands to be irrevocably degraded by soil erosion thus is relatively small.

This assertion seemingly is supported by a number of recent socioeconomic studies (9, 10, 15). These studies suggest that soil erosion is not a major threat to long-term U.S. productive capacity. The analyses, moreover, involve assumptions about growth in U.S. agricultural exports that may or may not ever come to pass—and certainly will not until there is recovery and substantial growth in the world economy.

This is not to suggest that soil erosion and runoff are trivial problems. Indeed, the evidence suggests that the off-farm costs of erosion and runoff are substantial. More importantly, the costs likely exceed the on-farm costs. There are, to be sure, inadequate data on the on-farm and off-farm costs of soil erosion and runoff. But the following numbers may give some idea of the relative magnitudes involved.

One estimate of erosion's threat to long-term soil productivity suggests that if current rates of erosion persist the result will be the destruction of about 27 million acres of cropland over the next 50 years (19). This is roughly 500,000 acres per year on the average, which no doubt is less than the acreage of prime farmland that will be lost annually through conversion to urban uses. At $1,000 per acre, a generous figure given the generally marginal, steeply sloped land involved, and ignoring the complications of changing land prices and discounting, the loss would be about $500 million annually. By comparison, estimates of annual sedimentation costs in rivers, harbors, reservoirs, and lakes alone have been put at $1 billion (*11, 24*). There are further paid and unpaid costs of erosion and runoff in the areas of water pollution control, health problems from contaminated water supplies, increased salt loading of streams, and so forth that would increase this figure substantially.

One is thus compelled to conclude that soil erosion and surface and subsurface transport of agricultural chemicals and other substances are primarily problems of water resource degradation that have added consequences for long-term land productivity, rather than vice-versa. What are the implications of this conclusion? There are three primary ones.

One is that there has been an asymmetrical relationship between the themes and foci of public policy and educational programs and the actual socioeconomic dimensions of soil and water conservation problems. Programs have long emphasized that agricultural resource degradation is primarily a concern because of the long-term loss of soil resources. In fact, the loss of soil resources is probably less costly to society than are the impacts on water quantity and quality.

A second implication is that this conceptualization of the soil and water problem has diverted the attention of researchers and policymakers from the possibility that regulation may be the only effective way to deal with erosion and runoff problems. This observaton is offered as a warning, not as a point of advocacy. As the political efficacy of farm organizations is weakened through the continued decline of farmers and solidarity among farmers, interest groups outside of farming will promote and may be able to facilitate legislation requiring such agencies as SCS and the Environmental Protection Agency to regulate the conservation of soil and water.

The third implication is that the traditional conceptualization has reinforced social science scholarship toward emphasizing micro levels of analysis. If the task of soil and water conservation is to encourage farmers to adopt soil and water conservation innovations because these innovations are in farmers' long-term interests, micro approaches to research clearly would yield greater understanding of these problems and public policy remedies. But the available data on the relative on-farm and off-farm costs of soil erosion and runoff of agricultural chemicals and other substances suggest that, to some degree at least, these problems are macro ones in one sector—production agriculture—externalizing substantial costs to the rest of society.

Farm Structure and Natural Resource Degradation

Continued degradation of soil and water resources because of production agriculture is associated with historic conditions in U.S agriculture. These conditions have led to greater concentration of farming and, in part, to the recent financial crisis in farming. Generally, it is agreed that the immediate crux of the soil and water conservation problem is that the practices to achieve conservation often are not privately profitable. There is also general agreement about why this is the case.

First, because of product price instability and increasingly inflexible cost structures in farming, agricultural producers tend to have short-term planning horizons. If a farmer is mainly concerned with survival of the enterprise from one year to the next, immediate returns are more valuable than the long-term returns from resource conservation. Economic insecurity thus causes farmers to discount heavily the long-term benefits of soil and water conservation.

Second, agriculture, as an industry, is generally characterized by a high degree of risk with regard to climatic and other natural vagaries. Farmers thus tend to avoid risk by using practices (e.g., prophylactic or subtherapeutic use of antibiotics in animal feed, excessive fertilization, preventive use of pesticides, irrigation) to minimize the impacts of these vagaries.   Finally, as implied earlier, farmers are able to externalize most of the costs of soil erosion and runoff so that the incentive for environmentally sound resource management is further weakened.

Recognizing these general parameters of farmer decision-making, such micro-level research has been concerned with whether structural characteristics of farm units account for differences in farmer behavior toward resource conservation. Many researchers have examined differential adoption of soil and water conservation innovations on the basis of such variables as farm size, tenure, juridical ownership form, and so forth. One hypothesis frequently explored is that family ownership and operation of farms are conducive to environmentally sound resource management. It is often hypothesized, for example, that owner-operated farms, as apposed to rented or absentee-owned farms, exhibit superior soil and water conservation practices. The results have been mixed (*17, 27*).

Another way to explore farm structure and agricultural resource management is at a macro level. This can be done in two related ways. The first involves some observations regarding the structural basis of the family farm. The second explores the dynamics of structural change in U.S. agriculture.

The longstanding family-farm heritage in the United States tends to lead scholars and policymakers to neglect crucial questions. Why does the family farm exist at all when virtually every other economic sector in advanced industrial societies has long since witnessed the demise of independent household ownership and operation of economic units? Why is agricultural production conspicuously less concentrated than the automobile, steel, chemical, pharamaceutical, fertilizer, and food-processing industries?

There are several reasons why family farms continue to exist and why agriculture is, on the whole, an industry with dispersed ownership structure. Moreover, these reasons for the persistence of family farming have major implications for resource management behavior in this sector.

First and foremost, agriculture, as an industry, is relatively unique because of the importance of land as its key capital input (3). The supply of land is essentially finite. It is, therefore, not feasible for this input to be manufactured, as is the case for the principal capital items in other industries. The finite land supply creates major barriers to the centralization of farm property. The computer industry, for example, can expand by purchasing the necessary capital goods that are manufactured in factories. But farmers can expand only by waiting for other farmers to sell or rent their land, a process that may take a long time.

Second, agricultural commodities on the whole tend to have low prices, based on the income elasticities of demand. This characteristic tends to result in market saturation, overproduction crises, and product price volatility. Each of these, individualy and collectively, has facilitated the historic tendency for greater concentration of production in U.S. agriculture.

Third, these economic risks are exacerbated by the risks associated with climatic and other natural vagaries.

Fourth, the tie of agriculture to the land resource and, hence, to vast reaches of geographical space limits the scale economies that are present in horizontal and vertical integration of production activities in other industries.

While agricultural production clearly has become more concentrated with few but larger farms, farming, for these reasons, tends not to be attractive for large-scale capital investment. Historically, production agriculture in the United States and in other advanced industrial societies has been relegated to household production units—family farms.

This brief structural analysis of the socioeconomic basis for the family farm has some interesting implications for agricultural resource management. First, the very characteristics of agriculture that lead to environmental degradation—product price instability, the cost-price squeeze, and high risk, short-term planning horizons—are solidly rooted in the structural basis of family farming (4). In other words, the characteristics of production agriculture that enable family farmers to resist the oligopolization and centralization process that has affected virtually all other major industries are those that lead farmers to underemphasize soil and water conservation practices.

Second, one must scrutinize the implicit notion of the "prosperous family farmer" that constitutes much of historic imagery of a long-term solution to soil and water degradation problems. The image typically conjured up in the literature is that the conservation behavior of American farmers would improve significantly if there were a structure of generally prosperous family farmers with capital to invest in conservation, longer term planning horizons, and the greater certainty of passing on the farm within the family. But one can see that, at least to some degree, the notion of a prosperous family farmer is a contradiction in terms. The structural basis of the family farm consists of factors that combine to produce low returns from agricultural investment. These same factors generally make agriculture unattractive for large-scale capital investment by nonfarm firms.

If agriculture were sufficiently profitable for widespread farmer prosperity to exist, family-farm units would ultimately be displaced by larger, industrial-type units. This is certainly the goal of current policy initiatives to make farming more responsive to international market conditions. This is not to suggest that the resource management behavior of industrial farms would necessarily be more benign than that of a dispersed system of owner-operated farms. The incentive would still exist for growers to externalize the costs of land degradation. But it is worth noting that society would likely be far less tolerant of soil erosion and runoff problems in a farm sector consisting largely of industrial-type farms. It would probably be far easier to implement mandatory regulation of agricultural practices if there were not a countervailing symbolic constraint: the struggling, financially strapped family farmer who should not be regulated into bankruptcy.

How does structural change affect resource management in agriculture? The basic features of post-world War II structural change in agriculture—fewer and larger farms, mechanization, increased capital intensity, enterprise and regional specialization, and so on—are widely recognized. There is no need to examine them in detail here. Instead, there is need to focus on two key structural paradoxes in American agriculture vis-a-vis resource management. These paradoxes imply that the forces of structural change in agriculture will tend to overwhelm approaches to soil conservation that rely on influencing farmer decision-making through cost-sharing, technical assistance, and education.

The first paradox centers around the fact that the dominant thrust of structural change in U.S. agriculture—increased scale, growing concentration, increased mechanization, increased capital intensity, increased use of hired labor—has corresponded with agronomically related changes in the direction of enterprise and regional specialization, the separation of crop and livestock production between farms and over space, and intensification of production (31). For example, several researchers have demonstrated how expansion in farm size has tended to be accompanied by mechanization, which, in turn, has led to enterprise specialization as a means of reducing per unit costs by spreading the fixed costs over larger acreages (12, 30). The result has been long-term trends toward row-crop and small grain monocultures; a reduced prevalence of crop rotation, particularly those involving legumes; separation of crop from livestock production; and the intensificiation of crop production based on purchased petrochemical inputs. Each of these agronomically related trends is adverse for controlling environmental externalities in agriculture (2, 16, 20, 24). Long-standing structural trends in American agriculture thus put formidable constraints on the ability to reduce soil erosion and the surface and subsurface transport of chemicals off farms.

But while the trend toward larger, specialized farms has increased the barriers to effective agricultural resource management, micro-level research tends to confirm the paradoxical generalization that it is on these farms that one is more likely to find the adoption of soil conservation innovations and the lowest soil loss rates (8, 13, 21, 23). This positive relationship between farm size or farm income and conservation behavior, typically measured in terms of adoption of conservation tillage, has a relatively straightforward explanation. First, farm size and income are "indicators of the ability to make an investment" in conservation tillage equipment (23). Second, such investments in erosion control hardware were, when these studies were conducted, heavily subsidized by the U.S. tax system. Tax subsidies to capital investment were especially attractive to larger operators in higher income brackets. These tax subsidies remain in effect, but they are attractive only when farmers are in high income tax brackets, a relatively rare situation today for most producers of row crops and small grains. Finally, and perhaps most importantly, conservation tillage machinery is a more labor-saving innovation than it is merely a conservation innovation. Conservation tillage practices substantially reduce labor inputs during the critical planting season and, accordingly, serve to increase the timeliness of tillage operations (2, 26). Labor-saving technology may be especially attractive on large farms, where the labor hired constitutes a cash expense.   There is some evidence that farmers have adopted such soil conservation innovations as a result of positive personal attitudes toward conservation (22, 23, 27). But it is likely that these innovations would have been adopted with or without pro-conservation value motivations because conservation tillage conforms so clearly to post-World War II structural trends toward adoption of labor-saving mechanical technology, farm enterprise specialization, and intensification of production through the use of petrochemicals in the form of herbicides (2). Moreover, there exists evidence that larger farm operators are less likely than smaller farmers to believe that soil conservation and pollution from agricultural runoff are important problems and to support expanded governmental efforts to reduce erosion and runoff (6).

The second paradox of farm structure and agricultural resource conservation relates to the cyclical nature of the agricultural economy. As noted earlier, this cyclical nature tends to be inherent in the farming industry. Interestingly, Emery Castle in the proceedings of a symposium, *Future Agricultural Technology and Resource Conservation* (7), offered a crucial argument, in apologetic tones, about the environmental consequences of agricultural instability:

"To some it may seem that it is going rather far afield to mention macro-economic policies in relation to agricultural land use. Certainly this is not the place to trace out all of these relationships. Suffice it to say that an unstable economic environment does not work in favor of soil conservation. Inflationary periods when interest rates fail to reflect anticipated price increases encourage land speculation rather than interest in land as a productive asset. Depressed economic conditions, on the other hand, place economic pressure on the farmer for short-run survival. Greater stability in the economy generally would make a substantial contribution to better land use."

In that same book a comparable argument was made somewhat less apologetically:

"The cost-price squeeze tends to be cyclical; in good years, farmers tend to bid their above normal incomes into existing asset markets, resulting in land price inflation and in consequent rises in cost equilibria (which set the stage for the next phase of the cost-price squeeze). Yet the micro phenomenon of cost-price squeeze is not the only factor that affects agricultural resource management. Rising relative land prices dictate the adoption of land-saving technologies (e.g., petrochemicals as substitutes for crop rotations and animal manures), thereby undermining the traditional practices which conserved soil in the past.... The crucial relationship between the micro and macro levels of analysis in this perspective is a contradictory one; enhancing farmers' incomes to solve the problem of short-term planning horizons caused by the cost-price squeeze will exacerbate the macro, land-related circumstances (capitalization of incomes in asset values, and enterprise and regional specialization) which have contributed to agricultural resource degradation" (4).

Dealing With the Policy Contradiction

There are several additional observations to offer on the paradoxical ratcheting-up of environmental degradation in agriculture. First, the inherent tendency toward instability in the agricultural economy notwithstanding, much of the thrust of federal commodity price supports and other government programs (Public Law 480, government stockpiling of surplus commodities, and so on) historically has been to reduce instability in the agricultural economy (*14, 28*). Second, commodity progams of late have been ineffective in reducing this instability. In fact, data for 1976-1981 indicate that commodity programs have tended to increase instability in farm income (*28*). Over the past decade, as U.S. agriculture has been more closely integrated into the world agricultural economy and as target prices and price-support levels have moved closer to declining world market prices, commodity programs have become subordinate to fiscal, monetary, and trade policies as determinants of farm income instability.

The farm crisis that currently afflicts American agriculture dramatizes the declining ability of the federal government to attenuate instability in the agricultural economy. The massive decapitalization of agriculture, staggering debt load, and internationalization of the U.S. farm economy in a milieu of depressed commodity prices, stagnation of export sales, high real interest rates, and the overvalued U.S. dollar have combined to place farming in its worst financial crisis since the Great Depression. Commodity programs, as costly as they have been to the U.S. treasury in recent years, have failed to place a floor under farm commodity prices and thereby avoid the startling erosion of farm asset values. Thousands of farmers have gone bankrupt or face the prospect of bankruptcy over the next year or two. Progress in soil and water conservation is basically at a standstill because most farmers are reluctant or unable to invest in anything other than essential capital items. These conditions are likely to change with recovery in the world economy, increases in world farm commodity prices, and declines in real interest rates. Moreover, with farm asset values having been depreciated to a level closer to their ability to generate net farm income at or about the average level of profit in the general economy, the stage will be set for a dramatic expansion of the agricultural economy: rising real estate values spurred by tax incentives, land speculation, and declining interest in land as a productive asset (*7*). This new, increased capital intensity in agriculture will be conducive to resource conservation only to the degree that there is further development of labor-saving tillage equipment with the auxiliary potential to reduce erosion and runoff.

This scenario, of course, is not inevitable. The path followed will be largely shaped by public policy and, to a lesser extent, by future technological change. The point, however, is that, in what promises to be an increasingly volatile agricultural economy over the next decade, progress in soil and water conservation may be determined more by general agricultural policy, including tax and monetary-fiscal policies that affect the entire economy, than by conservation policy. Those who remain concerned about the environmental performance of U.S. agriculture will need to devote more effort to understanding how agricultural policy and farm structural change affect farmer decision-making about natural resources.

A more rational agricultural policy—on social, fiscal, and economic grounds—might also contribute to better resource management by American farmers. The present is an ideal time to reconsider U.S. agricultural policy. Current programs are expensive and ineffective. There is a rekindling of concern about the future of the family farm as well. Perhaps by the next presidential election there will be a sufficient groundswell of opinion to restructure agricultural policy in ways as revolutionary as those during the Great Depression. Moreover, it may be plausible to design new policies that will bolster the status of the family farm while simultaneously creating conditions more suitable for resource conservation. Two potentially large constituencies—groups supporting the family farm and those favoring environmental protection—could be mobilized to make far-reaching policy changes.

Soil and water degradation is associated with the contradiction of agricultural production. Various interest groups and government agencies have called attention to high rates of soil erosion. Some compare the current crisis to that during the Great Depression. But during the last four years, the SCS budget has been reduced significantly. It is unreasonable to expect the agency's voluntary programs to succeed in the face of unfavorable farm economic conditions. To blame SCS for not curbing soil erosion is tantamount to blaming a fire department for not putting out a fire when the water pressure in its hoses is too low.

If soil and water regulations at the farm level are to be avoided, SCS must receive higher fiscal allocations than currently is the case. While it may seem unpopular to recommend budget increases at this time, the evidence suggests that money invested in voluntary farmer compliance may save money spent on the clean-up of off-site pollution. Micro targeting, a continuing program of SCS, offers an efficient way of allocating scarce resources. It would be an expensive irony to undercut voluntary farm-level conservation efforts only to pay more eventually for off-site clean-up and the enforcement of regulatory conservation programs.

Policymakers must take into account macro-socioeconomic factors that constrain farmers from practicing soil and water conservation. In so doing, policymakers must also take a closer look at the usefulness of social science research.

REFERENCES

1. Badie, B., and P. Birnbaum. 1983. *The sociology of the state.* University of Chicago Press, Chicago, Illinois.
2. Batie, S. S. 1983. *Soil erosion: Crisis in America's croplands?* The Conservation Foundation, Washington, D.C.
3. Buttel, F. H. 1983. *Beyond the family farm.* In G. F. Summers [editor] *Technology and Social Change in Rural Areas.* Westview Press, Boulder, Colorado. pp. 87-107.
4. Buttel, F. H. 1984. *Discussion.* In B. O. English, et al. [editors] *Future Agricultural Technology and Resource Conservation.* Iowa State University Press, Ames. pp. 269-275.

5. Buttel, F. H. 1984. *Socioeconomic equity and environmental quality in North American agriculture.* In G. K. Douglass [editor] *Agricultural Sustainability in a Changing World Order.* Westview Press, Boulder, Colorado. pp. 89-106.
6. Buttel, F. H., G. W. Gillespie, Jr., O. W. Larson III, and C. K. Harris. 1981. *The social bases of agrarian environmentalism: A comparative analysis of Michigan and New York farm operators.* Rural Sociology 46 (fall): 391-410.
7. Castle, E. N. 1984. *Land use.* In B. O. English, et al. [editors] *Future Agricultural Technology and Resource Conservation.* Iowa State University Press, Ames. pp. 98-110.
8. Choi, H., and C. M. Coughenour. 1979. *Socioeconomic aspects of no-tillage agriculture: A case study of farmers in Christian County, Kentucky.* Report RS-63. Department of Sociology, University of Kentucky, Lexington.
9. Crosson, P. R. 1982. *The long-term adequacy of agricultural land in the United States.* In P. R. Crosson [editor] *The Cropland Crisis: Myth or Reality?* Johns Hopkins University Press, Baltimore, Maryland. pp. 1-22.
10. Crosson, P. R., with A. T. Stout. 1983. *Productivity effects of cropland erosion in the United States.* Resources for the Future, Washington, D.C.
11. Crosson, P. R., and S. Brubaker. 1982. *Resource and environmental effects of U.S. agriculture.* Resources for the Future, Washington, D.C.
12. Dovring, F., and J. F. Yanagida. 1979. *Monoculture and productivity: A study of private profit and social product on grain farms and livestock farms in Illinois.* AE-4477. Department of Agricultural Economics, University of Illinois, Urbana.
13. Earle, T. R., C. W. Rose, and A. A. Brownlea. 1979. *Socioeconomic predictors of intention towards soil conservation and their implications in environmental management.* Journal of Environmental Management 9: 225-236.
14. Farrell, K. R. 1983. *Commodity programs: Discussion.* American Journal of Agricultural Economics 65 (December): 935-936.
15. Gardner, B. D. 1985. *Government and conservation: A case of good intentions but misplaced incentives.* In S. B. Lovejoy and O. C. Doering [editors] *Government and Conservation: What Should Be the Role of Government?* Department of Agricultural Economics, Purdue University, West Lafayette, Indiana.
16. Heady, E. O. 1984. *The setting for agricultural production and resource use in the future.* In B. O. English, et al. [editors] *Future Agricultural Technology and Resource Conservation.* Iowa State University Press, Ames. pp. 8-30.
17. Hooks, G. M., T. L. Napier, and M. V. Carter. 1983. *Correlates of adoption behaviors: The case of farm technologies.* Rural Sociology 48 (summer): 308-323.
18. Kolko, G. 1961. *The triumph of conservatism.* Quadrangle, Chicago, Illinois.
19. Larson, W. E., F. J. Pierce, and R. H. Dowdy. 1983. *The threat of soil erosion to long-term crop productivity.* Science 219: 458-465.
20. Larson, W. E., F. J. Pierce, and R. H. Dowdy. 1984. *Our agricultural resources: Management for conservation.* In B. O. English, et al. [editors] *Future Agricultural Technology and Resource Conservation.* Iowa State University Press, Ames. pp. 40-59.
21. Miller, W. L. 1982. *The farm business perspective and soil conservation.* In H. G. Halcrow, et al. [editors] *Soil Conservation Policies, Institutions and Incentives.* Soil Conservation Society of America, Ankeny, Iowa.
22. Napier, T., and D. L. Forster. 1982. *Farmer attitudes and behavior associated with soil erosion control.* In H. G. Halcrow, et al. [editors] *Soil Conservation Policies, Institutions, and Incentives.* Soil Conservation Society of America, Ankeny, Iowa.
23. Nowak, P. J. 1984. *Adoption and diffusion of soil and water conservation practices.* In B. O. English, et al. [editors] *Future Agricultural Technology and Resource Conservation.* Iowa State University Press, Ames. pp. 214-237.
24. Pimentel, D., et al. 1976. *Land degradation: Effects on food and energy resources.* Science 194: 149-155.
25. Rosenbaum, W. 1973. *The politics of environmental concern.* Praeger, New York, New York.
26. Swanson, L. E. 1981. *Reduced tillage technology and Kentucky small farmers.* Culture and Agriculture 12 (August): 1-5.
27. Swanson, L. E., and J. F. Thigpen, III. 1984. *Kentucky farmers' attitudes and*

behavior toward conservation. Community Issues 6(2): 1-7.
28. Tweeten, L. 1983. *Economic instability in agriculture: The contributions of prices, government programs, and exports.* American Journal of Agricultural Economics 65 (December): 922-931.
29. Wessel, J., with M. Hantman. 1983. *Trading the future.* Institute for Food and Development Policy, San Francisco, California.
30. White, T. K., Jr., and G. D. Irwin. 1972. *Farm size and specialization.* In A. G. Ball and E. O. Heady [editors] *Size, Structure, and Future of Farms.* Iowa State University Press, Ames. pp. 190-213.
31. Youngberg, I. G., and F. H. Buttel. 1984. *Public policy and sociopolitical factors affecting the future of sustainable farming systems.* In *Organic Farming: Current Technology and Its Role in a Sustainable Agriculture.* American Society of Agronomy, Madison, Wisconsin. pp. 167-185.

4

Interorganizational Relations in Conservation Targeting Programs

James Nielson

In 1981 the U.S. Department of Agriculture (USDA) launched a national program to target conservation efforts in critical resource areas. The decision to pursue this approach to conservation goals resulted from observations that many natural resource problems are concentrated in limited geographic areas. Normally, USDA's conservation efforts are spread widely and uniformly throughout the nation's agricultural areas. While targeting is a department-wide initiative, the key agencies in designing and implementing the program are the Soil Conservation Service (SCS) and Agricultural Stabilization and Conservation Service (ASCS).

Beginning in 1981, USDA's Agricultural Research Service (ARS) and Economic Research Service (ERS) designed and carried out a research project on targeting. Project objectives were to analyze (1) the delivery system used in implementing the targeting program; (2) the change in farmers' use of recommended soil erosion control practices and factors associated with adoption; and (3) the impacts of targeting on farm income, long-term agricultural productivity, and sediment reduction.

SCS and ASCS targeted programs for several purposes. The ARS and ERS research addressed only programs for controlling water erosion on cropland—the resource problem with the highest priority on USDA's agenda and the one receiving the largest proportion of targeted funds and personnel. ARS and ERS concentrated on targeting in which SCS provided accelerated technical assistance and ASCS provided additional cost-sharing to help farmers apply soil erosion control practices.

The targeting program was studied in detail in four states, one in each of the four major water erosion areas USDA targeted in 1981. These four states were Alabama in the Coastal Plain, Missouri in the Corn Belt, Tennessee in the Mississippi Valley Uplands, and Washington in the Palouse area of the Pacific Northwest. A total of 709 farmers were interviewed on a random basis in two counties in each of the four states. Detailed case studies of the targeting program were also conducted in the four states and eight counties. Less detailed studies of the targeting programs were conducted in nine other states.

In addition to the farm survey data, information used in the research came from personal interviews with SCS and ASCS personnel at the county, area, state, and national levels; personal interviews with Extension personnel; personal interviews with others from the executive and legislative branches of the federal government and representatives of conservation organizations; phone interviews with samples of SCS and ASCS personnel in targeted and nontargeted counties; and records, reports, and data bases of SCS and ASCS at county, state, and national levels. The research focused on the period 1981-1983 or about the first two and one-half years of the USDA targeting effort.

In planning the research ARS and ERS had a great deal of interaction with the conservation agencies, especially SCS, but to a substantial extent with ASCS also. Among many other things, ARS and ERS studied the annual SCS reports, *Soil and Water Conservation Research* and *Educational Progress and Needs.*

The research was designed to meet the information needs of those who make policy, program, and budget decisions on conservation efforts, primarily in the federal government. The objective was to provide information useful in making near-term adjustments in targeting to improve its organization and management and in longer term policy development and program planning.

Five reports based on the research are being published: a basebook, an analysis of the delivery system used in implementing the program, what adoption of soil erosion control practices occurred, economic impacts of targeting, and major findings and implications. These reports generally outline what happened; present the findings; and offer suggestions for improving program design implementation and policy formulation. Suggestions focus on targeting as much as possible, but because the targeting effort blended in so closely with the base programs on which they were built, some analyses apply to conservation programs generally.

Interorganizational Relations Among Federal Agencies

While the research concentrated on SCS and ASCS, some information was gathered on Extension.

SCS-ASCS Relations.   SCS selected the initial target areas and launched the targeting program from the national level in 1981. While targeting coincided with the National Conservation Program, which had been developed in cooperation with other USDA agencies and with broad public participation, SCS initiated the program with relatively little consultation with ASCS or other agencies. SCS administrators moved ahead because they believed in targeting and had received some new discretionary funds they could use for this purpose.

ASCS joined the national targeting effort in 1982. The agency put additional cost-sharing funds into the same counties SCS had targeted in 1981. ASCS was involved informally in making the final selections of areas to be targeted by both agencies for the first time in 1983. Starting with areas to be targeted in 1984, selections were made jointly by SCS and ASCS on the basis of proposals submitted by the state offices of the agencies. Because of budget constraints and other reasons, ASCS did not target all of the counties targeted by SCS.

In almost all cases SCS took the lead in developing the proposals. State SCS offices varied in the extent to which they involved ASCS, other agencies, county staffs, and local groups. In some cases ASCS was deeply involved from the beginning. In other cases ASCS was involved only minimally and/or belatedly. Even where ASCS had little involvement in preparing proposals, the agency agreed that SCS had picked the right areas to target. Where ASCS staff members were not involved, some said they really didn't mind; others made it clear that they did.

At the state level there was a great deal of interaction between the state SCS and ASCS offices in implementing the targeting effort in many states. There was often close cooperation as well in allocating resources to targeted counties. In Alabama the decision to use all targeted cost-share funds for long-term agreements was made jointly.

When considering SCS-ASCS relationships at the county level, it is useful to note that in the study counties, on average, there was a 50 percent increase in both SCS staff and ASCS cost-sharing funds under targeting. The increase in cost-sharing funds required considerable interaction between ASCS and SCS in handling referrals of applications from farmers for cost-sharing funds. This situation presented the possibility for closer working relationships, but it also created potential problems as well.

When a farmer applies to ASCS for cost-sharing, the application typically is referred to SCS, which does a needs and feasibility analysis on the practices the farmer proposes to apply. If the county committee approves the application, funds are obligated to the farmer, and SCS is asked to assist the farmer with design and layout of the practices. Once the work is completed, SCS checks the work and, if done properly, certifies that the practices have been installed according to specifications. ASCS then pays the cost-sharing funds to the farmer.

A number of SCS district conservationists indicated that they had reached some farmers for the first time through the referral work. They used these contacts with farmers as an opening to encourage them to do more conservation planning. In some cases they motivated farmers to adopt conservation practices by telling them about the increased cost-sharing funds available from ASCS under the targeting program.

In most targeted counties studied both SCS and ASCS staffs reported that there was a moderate to heavy increase in SCS workload to handle referrals under targeting. ASCS acknowledged that it had had occasional complaints from farmers who felt SCS had not handled the referral work fast enough. But most states reported that the problem was a temporary one, troublesome only during the first year that ASCS had additional cost-share funds. After that referrals became less of a problem because SCS caught up with the workload; because SCS brought in temporary staff to handle the workload; or, in at least one state, because ASCS offices adopted a new procedure for moving applications to SCS more rapidly, rather than accumulating them and sending them in large batches.

Beginning in 1983 some county ASCS committees asked SCS to provide information on CRES Form AD-862 regarding the estimated soil loss with and without the proposed practices. (CRES stands for Conservation Reporting and Evaluation System, a system developed and used cooperatively by ASCS and SCS.) In one state interviewees said that using the form led to conflicts between the agencies. But much more often working together on the CRES system reportedly led to closer relationships, which in fact was an objective the agencies had in mind in developing the system.

The Extension Role. In some counties Extension personnel were deeply involved in and provided effective support for the targeting program. For example, Extension took the leadership for the resource conservation management farms that became a part of the targeting program in Tennessee. Extension, SCS, ASCS, and TVA cooperated closely on this project. In the Green Hills area of Missouri an Extension specialist assisted with the identification of leaders and conservation problems in initiating the targeting program. That same individual generally worked closely with SCS and ASCS on the program. Extension, SCS, and other organizations also cooperated in sponsoring conservation tours and field days in targeted areas of a number of states.

In other cases Extension was only passively or minimally involved in the targeting effort. In two states SCS officials said they had attempted to get Extension involved in the program and had even offered to pay the salaries of Extension personnel to assist in the program, but had gotten no response.

Two fairly basic problems were observed at the organizational interface between Extension and the conservation agencies. One related to whom should take the lead on conservation information and education programs. The ARS and ERS research showed that one of the important things that happened during the first two years of the targeting effort was that farmers became more aware of soil erosion problems and the need to do something about those problems. In most cases farmers became more aware as a result of SCS activities, sometimes with cooperation from Extension, often without.

Almost everyone involved in the study agreed that information and education are appropriate functions for Extension. But in many cases Extension was not staffed or not in tune with making conservation education a significant part of its program. A number of SCS employees contended that Extension was primarily a production-oriented agency and left leadership on conservation matters to SCS. Some Extension staff accepted this as a reasonable assessment. Others did not. Obviously, there is room for variation in the division of labor on information activities between Extension and SCS depending on staff size, capabilities, and interests.

A second problem between Extension and the conservation agencies related to conservation tillage. About 10 years ago SCS pushed ahead with promoting conservation tillage while Extension was cautious about supporting the practice. A 1977 General Accounting Office report (3) and many SCS personnel saw Extension's slowness in supporting conservation tillage as a national problem that damaged the conservation effort in general and targeting in particular. Where Extension did not support conservation tillage, various reasons were given: more research and proof were needed before the agency could recommend it; weed, insect, and disease problems associated with increased residues under conservation tillage made it questionable as to whether the practice was feasible; and in the Pacific Northwest, where SCS recommended planting wheat early in the fall to get cover on the ground, Extension recommended planting later to avoid disease problems.

In many areas Extension now supports conservation tillage, and a number of SCS officials credit Extension with being especially helpful in educating farmers on crop varieties and use of herbicides needed to make conservation tillage work successfully.

As a general view of conservation, some SCS staff indicated that Extension underemphasized soil loss and overemphasized economics, management, and profitability of practices. That seems doubtful. At the same time, SCS staff acknowledged that many SCS personnel overemphasized soil loss and underemphasized economics and profitability of practices, which sounds believable.

More on SCS-ASCS Relations. In some targeted areas it would be fair to say that SCS and ASCS cooperatively planned and executed the targeting program. But overall it is more nearly correct to say that SCS and ASCS planned and implemented their phases of targeting independently.

Farmers did not see the agencies as having a unified program. A few said they thought the targeting effort would be improved if it were put under one agency.

On the other hand, the ARS and ERS study indicated that the two agencies reinforced each other to a rather high degree in carrying out the targeting program. The two agencies generally pursued the same objectives in targeting, and there was considerable interaction between them through referrals of farmers and in other ways. One must be impressed by the number of SCS staff who said that ASCS cost-sharing was the key factor in the success of targeting and by the number of ASCS staff who said nothing would have happened under targeting unless SCS had gotten out and stirred up interest.

Moreover, many county and state SCS and ASCS staffs said that working together in the targeting program had been instrumental in bringing about closer working relationships between the two agencies at both levels. One state ASCS staff person contended that the key to success in conservation is cooperation and that cooperation existed in that particular state. A member of an SCS state staff said the agency had needed something to help make its personnel work more closely with ASCS. Targeting had helped bring that about, and it provided the opportunity for both agencies to do even better in the future.

In some cases targeting also led to closer working relationships between Extension and the conservation agencies. For example, a district extension director in the Green Hills area of Missouri said that the relationship between SCS and Extension had improved dramatically and that it would never have happened without targeting. Given the sometimes stormy relationship between SCS and Extension in Missouri, this could be rated as a significant achievement (*1*).

Suggested Improvements. Two suggested improvements in particular emanated from the ARS and ERS research. The first improvement: Housing SCS, ASCS, and Extension personnel together would improve interagency cooperation.

The move toward county agricultural centers in the 1960s and 1970s was among the best innovations that has occurred in agriculture and conservation delivery systems. Proximity seems to promote cooperation. By wide odds, the most frequent interactions and closest working relations between SCS and ASCS—and the greatest involvement by Extension in the targeting efforts—occurred where USDA agencies were housed together.

Budget constraints may make it difficult to move further in the direction of housing agency personnel together in the near future (although cuts in personnel may conceivably facilitate this action). But whenever and wherever possible, housing agency personnel together will do much to increase the effectiveness of conservation efforts.

The second suggested improvement: SCS should involve ASCS, Extension, and other agencies earlier in the process of planning for targeting areas. Though SCS may take the lead, effective multiagency programs require early and in-depth involvement on the part of ASCS, Extension, and other agencies. It would not only promote better feelings, but it would lead to stronger support and more effective programs if ASCS and others were involved in decisions on which areas to target and in planning joint progams from the beginning.

Most targeted areas should receive accelerated technical and financial assistance, with the increased technical assistance preceding the increased cost-sharing. As mentioned earlier, ASCS did not target all of the areas that SCS targeted for cropland erosion control. There are some circumstances in which additional cost-sharing funds may not be needed as a component of a targeting program, for example, areas where the practices needed most to control soil erosion are not eligible for cost-sharing. But in most areas having additional cost-sharing funds as well as additional technical personnel will help motivate both agency personnel and farmers and result in a more effective conservation effort.

In the first 10 states targeted for cropland erosion control, counties received additional cost-sharing funds one year after the acceleration of the technical assistance program. The ARS and ERS analysis of acceleration and deceleration under targeting indicated that this was a correct decision—that acceleration of cost-sharing should lag acceleration of technical assistance by one to one and one-half years to allow time to build farmers' awareness and to carry out some conservation planning. But again, the program should be planned jointly from the beginning. This includes the rate and timing of inputs from each agency.

A number of conservation professionals stressed that a coordinated effort among USDA agencies will contribute to the success of conservation programs, whether targeted or not. In the farm survey a number of farmers perceived that the agencies were not always together, and the farmers were troubled by it. County personnel observed that farmers accept conservation practices better if they see a unified effort by all agencies and especially if they agree reasonably well on practice recommendations.

State and Local Involvement in Targeting

State Involvement. During the past decade there has been a trend toward greater involvement by state governments in conservation. State initiatives include soil erosion, sedimentation, and nonpoint pollution laws; increased appropriations for conservation; and state cost-sharing in about 18 states.

In most states various agencies and organizations supported the targeting program, some directly and some indirectly. For example, in Missouri the State Department of Conservation provided personnel to support the targeting effort. The State Department of Ecology supported the program in Washington.

The Iowa 2000 Project contributed indirectly to the targeting program in that state. Under this project each farmer in the state is to be contacted. Within five years of the contact, he or she must develop a conservation plan and then commit to implementing that plan within one year after the plan is developed.

Local Involvement. Involvement by local soil conservation district boards in planning and implementing the targeting program varied widely. Among the states studied, county and state SCS staff reported that some district boards had done one or more of the following in connection with targeting: helped set priorities for resource problems or practices to be emphasized in the program; selected geographic areas that were targeted within the county; identified farms or farmers that needed priority attention; and offered ideas for improving the program.

In some counties district supervisors contacted farmers, spoke at field days, and carried out other activities to help interest other farmers in conservation and in the targeting program. In Washington some supervisors provided equipment for no-till demonstrations and used their own planes to give people tours over conservation areas.

The state SCS office in Washington allocated targeted funds to conservation district boards under cooperative agreements for the boards to use in the targeting program. This approach had both advantages and disadvantages. On one hand, some SCS staff felt the cooperative agreements were the best tool they had ever had to get district boards to move out and do something on their own. They believed the cooperative agreements kept the boards enthused and involved, and they had more and better planned conservation efforts in the districts by virtue of the agreements. On the other hand, state staff expressed concern that agreements made it easy for districts to look at the agreements as their only source of funds and to no longer scramble for state and local funds.

Findings on State and Local Support. While some conservation district boards supported the targeting effort throughout the 1981-1983 period, they were in the minority. In telephone surveys ARS and ERS asked SCS district conservationists in targeted counties how much assistance they received from their district board in establishing the targeting program. District conservationists in nontargeted counties were asked how much help they received from the boards in carrying out their technical programs.

Fifty-six percent of the district conservationists in nontargeted counties said they had received much assistance from their boards, while only 23 percent of the district conservationists in targeted counties said they received help on their targeting programs. County and state SCS staff in a number of states reported that, while they had tried to get the boards to participate in the targeting program, much of the involvement had been rather superficial, consisting mainly of the boards reviewing and reacting to plans and progress reports. Moreover, some SCS staffs said the district boards were involved early in the program, but later seemed to lose interest. At least one state SCS staff person indicated that the agency's inability to get district boards involved was the biggest disappointment in the targeting program.

Conservation districts and state associations of conservation districts were in a unique position to support targeting and to use it as leverage to get more support for conservation. For the most part they chose not to do so. In some cases SCS district conservationists may simply have moved ahead without trying to involve the district boards.

Some boards in areas targeted in 1981 may not have gotten excited about the targeting program because additional funds were made available without any action or involvement on their part. After proposals were required, a number of boards became deeply involved in developing and promoting the proposals. Some boards and state associations of conservation districts may have seen targeting as a federal program in which they had little voice, and some may have philosophically opposed the concept of targeting.

The National Association of Conservation Districts (NACD) generally supported the concept of targeting, but strongly opposed the USDA targeting program unless it was supported by "new money" appropriated specifically for targeting. Because most funds for targeting came from redirected funds rather than from new appropriations, NACD actively campaigned against the targeting program in Congress and urged state and local organizations to do likewise. This stand by NACD likely affected state and local support for the targeting effort.

Suggested Improvements. Again, two suggested improvements emanated from the ARS-ERS research. The first involved strengthening the role of state and local conservation agencies in planning and implementing targeted programs, especially the role of conservation district boards.

It is not easy to arrive at a well-reasoned suggestion regarding the role of state and local conservation agencies in the targeting effort because targeting involves a mixture of federal, state, and local resources and priorities. Coordinating the program at all of these levels, especially given the interlinkages among the various levels, is essential to the success of the program, yet it has proved extremely difficult to manage.

Historically, USDA conservation programs have been decentralized. In the case of cost-sharing, county committees operated within national guidelines but they had a great deal of discretion on what practices would be funded and which farmers would receive cost-share funds. The work of SCS field offices is guided by the local conservation district boards, which are legal subdivisions of state government. The districts receive support for conservation programs from state and local governments. Many people regard this support and program management by farmers as one of the strengths of soil conservation institutions.

During the early 1980s, two trends produced a dilemma in the federal-state-local conservation partnership. On one hand, the National Conservation Program called for strengthening the role of the states in conservation programs. This was reinforced by the "New Federalism" policy of the administration that called for decentralizing responsibility and authority for allocating financial resources to nonfederal levels. To back up this philosophy, matching grants that were authorized in the 1981 Farm Bill and reaffirmed in the RCA process and National Conservation Program were to be made available to conservation districts through state conservation agencies. At the same time there was a trend toward centralization in USDA with increased central planning, coordination, and decision-making.

Some saw targeting as a sharp departure from the decentralized approach that had previously been the hallmark of USDA conservation programs. Under targeting, decisions are made at the national level on what criteria should be used, what areas are targeted, and how much technical assistance and cost-sharing resources will be allocated to them. The fact that SCS policy stated "our philosophy is to accelerate a local effort rather than initiate the effort" helped some, but not much.

Some believe that making federal conservation programs more effective will probably require more federal guidance. For example, Pierre Crosson and John Miranowski put it as follows:

"It must also be asked if improved targeting is consistent with the greater role for state and local agencies in setting conservation priorities. What is important to these agencies is not necessarily important from a national view. The perceived political imperative of serving essentially parochial interests has been a principal obstacle to better targeting all along. It is hard to see how institutional changes that would seem to strengthen these interests will promote improved targeting" (2).

For the targeting effort to be successful some national priorities and direction are necessary. The argument presented by Crosson and Miranowski certainly has some validity. One intermediate solution considered had the national offices allocating funds to state SCS and ASCS offices in line with resource problems and letting the state offices do the targeting. Few state SCS or ASCS staffs considered this a workable solution, however, primarily because of the political pressures on the state offices. The fact that state offices have had long-standing authority and encouragement to target problem areas and have done such a modest amount of it is probably sufficient evidence that some leverage from the national level is needed.

Part of the problem is that while state and county SCS and ASCS staffs are federal employees they become a part of the state and local organizational network. Not only do many members of the staffs become heavily oriented toward the local situation, but farmers and others come to look on these people as "theirs" and to become possessive of them. This has advantages, but it also creates problems. It created problems especially when nontargeted counties lost staff, as some did, or believed they did, because of targeting.

The targeting effort probably could be more effective if the balance of power were shifted to give state and local bodies more voice in planning and implementing programs. Progress in terms of participation in delivery-system activities and acceptance of erosion control practices was greater in areas where local boards were deeply involved in the targeting program.

State and local committees already are involved in decisions on what areas will be proposed for targeting. Their role could be strengthened by involving them earlier in pinpointing critical erosion areas; in deciding upon areas to recommend for targeting; in developing proposals; and, most importantly, in planning the program to fit local needs, in giving guidance to the targeting effort, and in evaluating the program and providing feedback for improving it.

It is helpful also if other state and local organizations are involved in and provide support for the program. These, of course, include state and local conservation organizations. But bankers, machinery dealers, chemical companies, and others can reinforce the program as well. In Tillamook County, Oregon, local creamery officials, following farm visits with SCS and ASCS staff, became convinced of the importance of conservation efforts, then regularly urged farmers to follow good conservation practices.

The second improvement to be made in terms of state and local involvement is to require more state and local financial support for targeting. This has drawbacks, of course. Overemphasis on state and local support as a criterion in allocating federal conservation resources sometimes is not consistent with the goal of concentrating federal resources in the most critical problem areas among agricultural states. Some agricultural states provide 25 times as much support for conservation from state and local sources as others. Coordinating inputs from the various levels might become more of a problem also. But requiring more financial support from state and local levels is consistent with the suggestion to strengthen the role of state and local conservation organizations.

The greatest progress under targeting occurred where there was a convergence of state and local funds with federal funds. This was the case to a substantial extent in both Missouri and Washington. This state and local support added leverage to the program. Where state and local groups contributed more of the financing, they had more of a voice in the program. With more at stake, they became more interested and involved.

State and local support can be used to hire technicians to help get practices on the ground, leaving the more technical work to SCS employees, which was an objective of the National Conservation Program. State cost-sharing can be of considerable value in motivating and helping farmers to adopt soil erosion control practices. Support from state and local levels can provide stability to the conservation effort. Pooling funds from various sources can also lend flexibility to program management. There are certain constraints on federal funds that do not apply to state and local funds, and vice versa.

During the past decade state and local support for soil and water conservation has increased more rapidly than federal support. That support grew from 13 percent of the total in 1973 to 24 percent in 1984. State and local governments are now more likely to be in position to increase their support for conservation than the federal government, at least in the immediate future.

REFERENCES

1. Childs, Michael K., and J. C. Headley. 1982. *Soil conservation and extension in Missouri: A study of conflict.* Journal of Soil and Water Conservation 37(4): 200-203.
2. Crosson, Pierre, and John Miranowski. 1982. *Soil protection: Why, by whom and for whom?* Journal of Soil and Water Conservation 37(1): 27-29.
3. U.S. Government Accounting Office. 1977. *To protect tomorrow's food supply, soil conservation needs priority attention.* CED-77-30. Washington, D.C.

II
Information Needs
and Dissemination

5

Information Needs
for Conservation Decisions

Jerald J. Fletcher and Wesley D. Seitz

A great deal of information is needed to make economically sound soil conservation policies in today's complex world. To understand the types and sources of this information, it is essential to consider the decision-making environment in which land users and policymakers operate.

Various characteristics of today's economic environment directly affect conservation decisions. Although interrelated, these characteristics can be loosely grouped in the following four categories of observations:

► *It's a Marginal World.* Individual producers are led by the "invisible hand" of the marketplace to make decisions based on the marginal effects of their actions on important outcomes. These outcomes are all those that directly affect the individual's welfare without significant nonmarket effects on other members of society. In any specific case the outcomes considered depend on the institutional environment and the definitions of individual property rights. As resources become scarce, society also tries to increase the efficiency of their use through public policy. The effect of such public action is to more closely align marginal benefits to marginal costs for public and private expenditures that affect both internal (primarily on-farm) and external (usually off-farm) effects at the farm level.

► *It's a Complex World.* Policies at all levels—local, state, and national—affect individual conservation decisions. Individual decisions also depend heavily on local conditions and often vary from area to area because of the uneven distribution of natural resources, climatic variation, and local markets. The off-site impacts of conservation decisions depend not only on physical variables but on the economic and social structures that are affected by such decisions. Decisions are also influenced by international markets. In addition, the multidisciplinary nature of conservation problems requires expertise from a range of specialties for adequate solution.

▶ *It's a Dynamic World.* There are times of surplus and times of shortage. The price signals that influence all production and investment decisions in a capitalistic or free market economy change constantly. Production technologies change. Even the institutional structures that affect individual and public conservation decisions are in a continual state of evolutionary and sometimes revolutionary change.

▶ *It's an Uncertain World.* Given the inherent variability in crop production and human behavior, it is always difficult and usually impossible to obtain the information required to make the best decisions during a relatively short time period. In addition, the decisions made by individuals depend not only on the average outcome in a given situation but on the degree and type of variability that is anticipated.

It's a Marginal World

Presumably, public and private decision-makers attempt to get the most "bang for the buck" for their conservation expenditures. As a result, they are inevitably led to decision rules based on marginal criteria. Many soil erosion-related problems, however, are often described in terms of average characteristics. Care must be taken not to confuse problems described with data based on average statistics with decisions that affect marginal activities.

Micro-Level Decisions. The decisions that individual land users make are guided by the marginal criteria from their frame of reference. From an economic perspective, we say that private decisions are not affected by externalities, that is those effects of the decisions that are not directly reflected in the production process or firm welfare. In cases characterized by either public "goods" (conservation) or public "bads" (soil erosion), an individual is not guided by the "invisible hand" to invest in conservation until his marginal cost is equated to society's marginal benefit. It is essential that this behavior be anticipated in the development of policies designed to limit soil erosion through changes in land use practices. It is especially important to understand the effects of conservation policies guided by social objectives on the farm firm and anticipate the reactions of the agricultural community which are based on individual welfare considerations to a variety of policy alternatives.

The lack of effectiveness of the traditional, structure-oriented conservation efforts by soil conservation agencies including the Soil Conservation Service and local conservation districts is a clear example of the failure to consider marginal economic criteria. The inability to get a significant proportion of land users to install and maintain structural measures on erodible land, even with substantial subsidies, indicates that the approach is not cost-effective from the farmers' perspective. In an Illinois study, for example, terraces were found not to be cost-effective even with a government cost-share of 50 percent (10).

One problem in designing cost-effective conservation measures has been the lack of information about the costs of soil erosion to the individual farmer and the benefits that might accrue to conservation investments. Two recent conferences attempted to stimulate research and to quantify known relationships about the effects of erosion on soil productivity. The first, held in Denver in 1983 and sponsored by the American Society of Agronomy, pointed out the lack of precision in techniques for determining the impacts of soil erosion on long-term productivity. A follow-up conference, sponsored by the American Society of Agricultural Engineers, was held in New Orleans in December 1984 (1). Four points of specific interest follow from the papers presented at these two meetings: (1) The effects of erosion on soil productivity is extremely site specific. (2) Productivity effects are, given available data, difficult to measure over a short time horizon and difficult to separate from the effects of changes in technology over a longer time frame. (3) Tolerable soil loss, the T value, does not adequately reflect the impact of soil loss on productivity. (4) Accurate estimates of the productivity costs of soil erosion are not yet available for the analysis needed to make most conservation decisions in the U.S.

Estimates of erosion's effect on productivity for various areas indicate that the damages are small (11).[1] Assuming such current research results are reasonably accurate, the lack of widespread adoption of conservation practices, especially relatively expensive structural measures, is understandable. While the effect of soil loss on potential productivity for a specific site may be high, only in rare instances will it be high enough to justify expensive control measures.

Do these observations imply that more recent attempts to influence the adoption of conservation tillage should meet with similar problems? Probably not, but for entirely different reasons. As a number of articles in the recent special issue of the *Journal of Soil and Water Conservation* on conservation tillage point out, conservation tillage is often cost-effective from a short-run perspective (14). That is, conservation tillage can be shown to increase farmers' profits without including the benefits from maintaining a higher level of long-term soil productivity or the

[1]Conclusion reached in a U.S. Department of Agriculture-sponsored "Forum on Erosion Productivity Impact Estimators" held May 8-9, 1985, in Arlington, Virginia.

benefits from improved environmental quality and reduced sediment loads. Therefore, we should realize that the impetus for adoption of "conservation" tillage is often driven by an economic rather than a conservation motivation.

A recent survey of farmers participating in an alternative tillage demonstration project in Indiana, Michigan, and Ohio found that more than three-fourths of the farmers said they either had or could obtain the necessary funding to invest in conservation tillage equipment.[2] Of those with access to funds, 81 percent said they would make the investment in conservation tillage equipment if they were convinced that conservation tillage was at least as profitable as conventional tillage. Together these answers imply, at least for this sample of farmers, that about five of eight will switch to conservation tillage when they are convinced it does

[2]Unpublished research results from a random survey of participants in the Lake Erie Accelerated Conservation Tillage Project, a cooperative effort by the U.S. Environmental Protection Agency, local conservation districts, Ohio Department of Natural Resources, and a number of other agencies. Conservation tillage in this project included only ridge-till and no-till systems. The survey research was sponsored by the Great Lakes National Program Office, EPA, under grant R005983-01 to Purdue University and by the Agricultural Experiment Station, Purdue University, under project IND 45099.

Table 1. Funds available and willingness to invest in conservation tillage equipment.

Question	Number of Responses*	Percent "Yes" (%)
Would funds, either internal or borrowed, be available to you to finance the machinery purchase necessary for you to change from conventional tillage to conservation tillage?	356	78
If you answered "yes" to the above question, and you were convinced that conservation tillage was at least as profitable as conventional tillage, would you use those funds available to you to make the switch in tillage systems?	268	81

Source: Unpublished preliminary research results from a 1985 survey of participants in the Lake Erie Accelerated Conservation Tillage Project. Conservation tillage in this project included only ridge-till and no-till systems. The survey research was sponsored by the Great Lakes National Program Office, U.S. Environmental Protection Agency, under grant R005983-01 to Purdue University and the Agricultural Experiment Station, Purdue University, under project IND 45099.
*A total of 396 surveys were returned. The number of responses is the number that had information on each question.

Table 2. Farmers' perspectives on profitability and tillage system change.

Question	Number of Responses*	Total	Cumulative
		%	
I would change to conservation tillage if the change in profitability were _____	347	100	
I will use conservation no matter what the costs are	42	12	12
Up to $20/acre less than conventional tillage	20	6	18
Up to $10/acre less than conventional tillage	48	14	32
Not different than conventional tillage	142	41	73
At least $10/acre greater than conventional tillage	39	11	84
At least $20/acre greater than conventional tillage	44	13	97
I would not change from conventional tillage	12	3	100

Source: Unpublished preliminary research results from a 1985 survey of participants in the Lake Erie Accelerated Conservation Tillage Project. Conservation
tillage in this project included only ridge-till and no-till systems. The survey
research was sponsored by the Great Lakes National Program Office, U.S. Environmental Protection Agency, under grant R005983-01 to Purdue University and
the Agricultural Experiment Station, Purdue University, under project IND
45099.
*A total of 396 surveys were returned. The number of responses is the number
  that had information on each question.

not hurt their bottom line (Table 1). Note that in this project the definition of conservation tillage was more restrictive than usual. Conservation
tillage included only no-till and ridge-till systems.

The same farmers were also asked to complete the sentence, "I would
change to conservation tillage if the change in profitability were
_____," from a number of discrete choices. About one-third said

[2]Unpublished research results from a random survey of participants in the Lake Erie
Accelerated Conservation Tillage Project, a cooperative effort by the U.S. Environmental
Protection Agency, local conservation districts, Ohio Department of Natural Resources,
and a number of other agencies. Conservation tillage in this project included only ridge-till
and no-till systems. The survey research was sponsored by the Great Lakes National Program Office, EPA, under grant R005983-01 to Purdue University and to the Agricultural
Experiment Station, Purdue University, under project IND 45099.

they would accept a penalty up to $10 per acre and still use conservation tillage. More than 70 percent indicated they would switch if the profitability were the same, and 84 percent said they would switch if there was a gain of $10 per acre. If the gain were $20 or more per acre, 97 percent indicated they would adopt conservation tillage (Table 2).

In an Indiana study comparing the profitability of alternative tillage systems, a group of tillage specialists at Purdue University found that at least one of these conservation systems—ridge-till or no-till—would give the $10-per-acre annual profit advantage for corn and soybean producers on most soils in Indiana (7). On highly erodible soils the conservation systems advantage would be $20 per acre or more.

Obviously, there remains a significant potential pay-off to information on the economic consequences of using conservation tillage in the Corn Belt. It is likely that similar results would hold for other regions of the United States as well.

A first information need is for an ability to assess the profitability of alternative, conservation-inducing tillage systems for specific sites and crops. Information need number two is for a method of generating site-specific estimates of erosion's potential effects on soil productivity.

Regional Impacts of Conservation Decisions. At the farm level, prices are taken as external or outside parameters. From a broader perspective, prices will change as individual firms adjust their production decisions. Changes in individual production decisons will further affect prices, production patterns, farm income, and demand for inputs at the farm and regional level until all changes have worked through the system to achieve a new balance.

In summarizing the results of studies dealing with the anticipated impacts of soil erosion control policies in the Corn Belt, Seitz and his co-authors stated: "Significant variations in economic impacts at the farm level and among regions can be expected as a result of the difference in the physical characteristic of farms." (*13*).

A third information need is to understand the regional impacts of alternative conservation decisions. This includes differences in production patterns, input demands, and net farm income among policy alternatives.

Off-farm Considerations. Information about the off-site impacts of soil erosion are also relevant for conservation decisons. This is especially true for conservation policy that must reflect the broader social concerns. Toby Clark outlines much of what is known (or estimated) about off-site costs in a recent book (*4*). An outline of his major points was included in the *Journal of Soil and Water Conservation* dealing with non-point water pollution (*3*).

A May 1985 conference organized by The Conservation Foundation outlined many of the information needs with respect to off-site impacts. Additional attention was drawn to this subject by the conference, "Perspectives on Nonpoint Source Pollution," held in May 19-22, 1985, in Kansas City, Missouri, and cosponsored by 40 private and public organizations.

Off-site impacts of erosion are a major justification for public input into soil conservation. The costs are not small. Clark estimates the off-site costs to be between $3 billion and $13 billion for the nation (4).

A recent study in Indiana by the Governor's Soil Resources Study Commission looked at the costs of removing sediment from road surfaces, roadside ditches, and regulated drains—costs not even considered in many studies of the effects of soil erosion (8). Three-fourths of the sediment was estimated to come from agricultural land (Table 3). Sediment removal costs totaled $11 million in 1983 (Table 4). This study estimated the total sediment related clean-up costs to be more than $500 million in Indiana and the annual costs to maintain roads and ditches in good condition to be more than $32 million (Table 5). If these costs are approximately correct, the off-site impacts of excessive erosion must be extremely high.

The fourth information need is to estimate the off-site costs of soil erosion that can be tied to farm-level characteristics and production practices.

There are significant research efforts underway to consider this aspect of conservation-related reseach needs. At the University of Illinois, Professor John Braden and colleagues are working on SEDEC, a modification of the SOILEC model, which includes sediment transport character-

Table 3. Sources of sediment (8). *

Source of Sediment	Percentage Sediment from Source (%)
Agricultural land	74
Roadsides	8
Streambanks	8
Urban areas	8
Other sources	2

*Results of 1984 survey of 92 Indiana counties. Sources of the sediment that accumulates on road surfaces and in roadside ditches and regulated drains and the average estimated percentage of the sediment from each source.

istics.[3,4] The purpose of this modeling effort is to develop a means of including the off-site impacts of conservation efforts in the development of small watershed conservation plans.

At Purdue University, a two-year research project is now underway to look at relationships between off-farm impacts of soil erosion and farm level production practices.[5] The net effect of such research efforts should be increasing awareness and understanding of soil erosion's costs to society.

It's a Complex World

International Trade Impacts. Modern agricultural policy analysis takes place in a complex environment. The harvests realized around the world dramatically affect the well-being of American farmers: the exchange rate may be the most important price in the world. No longer can international markets be ignored in domestic policy deliberations. Moreover, concern has been raised about the effects on the nation's natural resource base and environmental quality of farming fragile land to produce for the international market (6).

[3]Cooperative research effort by the University of Illinois and the Illinois Water Resources Center.
[4]Braden, J. B., and G. V. Johnson. 1985. "Efficiency of Sediment Control Policies." Agricultural economics staff paper. No. 85 E-311, University of Illinois. 9 pp.
[5]A cooperative research effort by Purdue University and the Soil Conservation Service. "Offsite Costs of Agricultural Production: A Framework for Analysis." Stephen B. Lovejoy and Jerald J. Fletcher, Department of Agricultural Economics, principal investigators.

Table 4. Estimated annual sediment removal expenditures in Indiana (8). *

Sediment Removal Site	1983 Cost	5-Year Average Cost
	——— ($1,000) ———	
Road surfaces	870 (9.4)	850 (9.2)
Roadside ditches	6,400 (70)	4,900 (53)
Total road costs	7,300 (79)	5,800 (63)
Regulated drains	3,800 (41)	3,800 (41)

*State totals are reported with county averages in parentheses.

Table 5. Estimated sediment removal expenditures for road surfaces, ditches, and regulated drains in Indiana (8). *

Sediment Removal Site	Cost for Total Clean-up	Cost Annually To Maintain
	———— ($1,000) ————	
Road surfaces	59,000 (640)	4,800 (52)
Roadside ditches	200,000 (2,100)	10,000 (110)
Total road costs	260,000 (2,800)	14,000 (160)
Regulated drains	260,000 (2,800)	18,000 (190)

*These figures represent the best estimates of a one-time cost to totally clean up and, thereafter, annually maintain the road surfaces, ditches, and regulated drains in Indiana. State totals are reported with county averages in parentheses.

Information need number five is to understand the effects of international trade on the soil resource base. How does conservation policy affect international trade? More importantly from a conservation perspective, what is the impact of international commerce on the effectiveness of conservation policies?

National, State, Local Policy Interaction/Coordination. Interest in soil erosion is now evident at all levels of government. The national interest is reflected in the Soil and Water Resources Conservation Act (RCA), the National Resources Inventory (NRI), and increasing interest in conservation-related policies. Three primary Corn Belt states, Iowa, Illinois, and Indiana, all have or have proposed soil erosion control goals that call for "T by 2000" (8, 9). Some counties in the Great Plains have enacted local legislation to prevent the plowing of fragile rangeland for wheat production.

A farmer feels the effects of actions taken at all levels of government. For efficiency, these policies should be coordinated and possible interactions considered. Policies that have significant interregional effects are appropriately established at the national level, while conservation-related problems that affect local areas and/or depend heavily on site-specific information are better dealt with at the local level. In some cases, the costs of policy implementation are greater than the benefits realized. In these cases no action is the appropriate response.

The sixth information need for any conservation policy is a full knowledge and understanding of existing policies at all levels as well as an understanding of the appropriate level for implementation and control.

Multidisciplinary Aspects of Conservation Policy. Development of appropriate conservation policies requires the input and knowledge of experts from a wide range of disciplines. Agronomists, hydrologists, engineers, soil scientists, entomologists, and climatologists are but a few of the physical science disciplines whose expertise may be required to evaluate specific conservation problems and policy alternatives. From the social sciences, political scientists may evaluate a proposed policy for political acceptability and implementability. The sociologist may consider aspects of social acceptability and adoption problems. The economist may offer input on efficiency and cost-effectiveness.

The seventh information need, therefore, is knowledge of the appropriate "place" to go for more input. Conservation problems are inherently multidisciplinary. An interdisciplinary approach to evaluation is thus critical to reach appropriate decisions.

It's a Dynamic World

Alternative Futures. The world is not static. As alternative policies are considered, the potential impacts for a variety of future scenarios must be analyzed.

One need not look far into the past to see significant changes in demand and supply interactions (*12*). The 1950s and 1960s were characterized by excess supply. Programs were developed to support prices and reduce supply. Some of these programs were coordinated with conservation goals. Overall, interest in conservation waned during this period. It seemed as though the soil erosion enemy had been met and vanquished by conservation efforts.

In the early 1970s, demand increased suddenly as the Soviet Union purchased large quantities of U.S. grain. The reaction of the agricultural sector to increased demand and higher prices was to increase supply. Fragile land was brought into production. Conservation-related structures, including terraces, waterways, and windbreaks installed over a number of years, were removed to increase short-run efficiency and output. Although these actions in part related to changes in production practices brought about by larger tillage and harvesting equipment, the need was driven by higher prices and production goals. Soil erosion on agricultural land again gained public exposure.

It is doubtful that farmers reacted directly to the secretary of agriculture's cry for increased production. They more likely reacted to increased prices. But the result was the same: Production went up; erosion went up; conservation went down! Many hard-earned gains made earlier were gone and the battle rejoined on different ground. Due in part to increased machinery size and pesticide effectiveness, the primary conservation tools have changed from structures, contouring, and rotations to conservation tillage.

The message from the past is clear. Information need number eight in making conservation decisions is to include the impacts of alternate future scenarios on the effectiveness of conservation policies. The specter of excessive stocks now confronts the nation, but for how long? It is cer-

Table 6. Expected yield change by tillage system.

	No-Till			Ridge-Till		
Question	Yield Change* (bu/ac)	Total (%)	Cumu-lative (%)	Yield Change† (bu/ac)	Total (%)	Cumu-lative (%)
Based upon your experiences	− 20	4	4	− 20	4	4
with tillage systems on soil	− 15	5	9	− 15	4	8
types common to your farm,	− 10	18	27	− 10	8	16
on the average, how do you	− 5	15	42	− 5	13	29
think no-till and ridge-till af-	0	27	69	0	38	67
fect corn yields compared to	+ 5	14	83	+ 5	20	87
your traditional tillage	+ 10	11	94	+ 10	9	96
system?	+ 15	3	97	+ 15	2	98
	+ 20	3	100	+ 20	2	100
Based upon your experiences	− 8	7	7	− 8	7	7
with tillage systems on soil	− 6	7	14	− 6	8	15
types common to your farm,	− 4	15	29	− 4	10	25
on the average, how do you	− 2	16	45	− 2	18	43
think no-till and ridge-till af-	0	33	78	0	29	72
fect soybean yields compared	+ 2	9	87	+ 2	13	85
to your traditional tillage	+ 4	7	94	+ 4	9	94
system?	+ 6	4	98	+ 6	5	99
	+ 8	2	100	+ 8	1	100

Source: Unpublished preliminary research results from a 1985 survey of participants in the Lake Erie Accelerated Conservation Tillage Project. Conservation tillage in this project included only ridge-till and no-till systems. The survey research was sponsored by the Great Lakes National Program Office, U.S. Environmental Protection Agency, under grant R005983-01 to Purdue University and the Agricultural Experiment Station, Purdue University, under project IND 45099.

*A total of 396 surveys were returned: 357 contained information on corn yield under no-till; 313 contained information on soybean yield under no-till.

†A total of 396 surveys were returned: 194 contained information on corn yield under ridge-till; 185 contained information on soybean yield under ridge-till.

tainly possible to realize a sudden reduction in international supply while demand continues to grow. How long will the current surplus situation last? What forces will move conservation policies when surpluses are exhausted?

Institutional Change. Neither political, legal, nor social institutions are stagnant. The legal environment depends on legislative initiatives, administrative implementations, and court decisions, all of which may reflect social attitudes (*15*). As the institutional structures in which decisions are made change, conservation policies must adapt to new requirements. Some policy alternatives that were not previously palatable to a majority of landowners may now be acceptable, or become so in the near future. For example, until recent years, cross-compliance among farm programs was viewed as an unacceptable alternative to most farmers and farm organizations. But research reported at a symposium on cross-compliance held as part of the 1983 American Agricultural Economics Association meeting indicated that cross-compliance is now considered a reasonable approach by many farmers and farm groups (*2*).

The need to understand the technical, political, social, legal, and economic feasibilities of alternative conservation decisions in policy development may be labeled information need number nine. Many of these points are more carefully addressed in other papers herein. The point here is that the potentially feasible policy or decision alternatives that must be considered for a specific problem tend to change over time.

Questions arise. What potential changes need to be considered? Will there be a movement from political boundaries at the local and regional levels (county and state) to more resource-based units (watershed and river basin)? Are cross-compliance options acceptable? Are mandatory options (standards) or tax (effluent-based) options acceptable? Will the owners of agricultural land assume, or be forced to assume, an obligation to protect soil productivity and/or minimize the off-site impacts of production?

It's an Uncertain World

The final attribute of our modern world that must be included in making conservation decisions is the uncertainty inherent in the outcomes associated with all decisions. Obviously, uncertainty is related to the attributes already discussed. The dynamic and complex nature of modern agriculture imposes uncertainty. The diversity of physical, social, and economic characteristics of farms leads to uncertainty on the part of individual producers and policymakers alike in anticipating the appropriate reaction to conservation policies.

But uncertainty is nothing new to agricultural producers. The impacts of the inherently variable nature of agricultural production processes on individual decisions have received a great deal of attention in agricultural economics literature. Assuming the average payoff to be the same, outcomes that have higher variability are considered less desirable than those with low variability. Even if the average increases, the effect on variability cannot be ignored in assessing the probable behavior of farmers. The pertinent question is how various conservation decisions may affect the uncertainty.

When considering the adoption of conservation tillage, for example, the relative variability in the profitability of conservation tillage systems compared with that of conventional tillage is an important factor. Farmers participating in the Lake Erie Accelerated Conservation Tillage Project were asked to compare the mean and variability of corn and soybean yields under conservation tillage (ridge-till or no-till) with that of their conventional system. Overall, farmers perceived ridge-till to have no significant impact on corn or soybean yields. Although the distribution of their expectations under the no-till system was centered around zero difference, it was skewed slightly toward a lower yield (Table 6). When

Table 7. Expected change in yield variation by tillage system. *

Question	No-Till Corn	No-Till Soybeans	Ridge-Till Corn	Ridge-Till Soybeans
			%	
Based upon your experiences with tillage systems on soil types common to your farm, how do you think no-till and ridge-till systems, on average, affect how yields vary from year to year compared to your present tillage system?				
Yield varies more	36	33	20	27
Yield varies the same	41	48	48	47
Yield varies less	23	19	32	26

Source: Unpublished preliminary research results from a 1985 survey of participants in the Lake Erie Accelerated Conservation Tillage Project. Conservation tillage in this project included only ridge-till and no-till systems. The survey research was sponsored by the Great Lakes National Program Office, U.S. Environmental Protection Agency, under grant R005983-01 to Purdue University and the Agricultural Experiment Station, Purdue University, under project IND 45099.

*A total of 396 surveys were returned: 332 contained information on corn yield variability under no-till; 292 contained information on soybean yield under no-till; 161 contained information on ridge-till corn; and 156 contained information on the variability of ridge-till soybeans.

comparing variability, no-till was thought to induce slightly greater variability, while ridge-till would reduce variability (Table 7). Based on these results, one would expect ridge-till to have a greater chance for acceptance than no-till. When asked directly to compare the profitability of two systems, however, a few more respondents expected a higher profit from no-till than from ridge-till (Table 8).

Obviously, even those farmers who have been exposed to a variety of tillage practices over the years have difficulty in comparing them direct-

Table 8. Farmers' perceptions of the profitability of no-till and ridge-till systems compared to traditional tillage.

Question	Number of Responses	Percent of Total	Cumulative Percentage
		%	
In your opinion, how profitable are the no-till and ridge-till tillage systems compared to the traditional tillage system you utilize?			
A no-till tillage system is _____ than my traditional tillage system			
$16 or more per acre less profitable	32	9	9
$6 to $15 per acre less profitable	66	18	27
No difference in profitability, within $5 per acre	121	32	59
$6 to $15 per acre more profitable	119	32	91
$16 or more per acre more profitable	35	9	100
A ridge-till tillage system is _____ than my traditional tillage system			
$16 or more per acre less profitable	13	7	7
$6 to $15 per acre less profitable	34	18	25
No difference in profitability, within $5 per acre	75	40	66
$6 to $15 per acre more profitable	48	26	91
$16 or more per acre more profitable	16	9	100

Source: Unpublished preliminary research results from a 1985 survey of participants in the Lake Erie Accelerated Conservation Tillage Project. Conservation tillage in this project included only ridge-till and no-till systems. The survey research was sponsored by the Great Lakes National Program Office, U.S. Environmental Protection Agency, under grant R005983-01 to Purdue University and the Agricultural Experiment Station, Purdue University, under project IND 45099.

*A total of 396 surveys were returned: 373 had answered the question on the profitability of the no-till system; 186 provided information on the ridge-till system.

ly. The tenth information need, then, is to understand the effects of alternative conservation policies on farm-level variability and decisions.

In Summary

A variety of information needs is appropriate for conservation policy formulation. These requirements can provide a guideline for future analysis of conservation policies. The information needs are as follows:

1. Marginal economic impacts of alternative conservation practices.

2. Site-specific estimates of soil erosion's impacts on productivity.

3. Regional impacts of alternative conservation decisions.

4. Estimates of the off-site costs of soil erosion on a per-farm basis.

5. Effects of international trade on soil resources.

6. Understanding existing and alternative conservation policies.

7. Appropriate information sources for input on conservation decisions.

8. Range of future scenarios in impact assessments.

9. Feasibility of conservation decisions and policies (technical, political, social, legal, and economic).

10. Effects of conservation policies on farm-level variability.

These points are neither exhaustive nor necessarily the most important for an economic analysis of a particular conservation problem or policy. But they indicate many requirements inherent in a variety of problems. The list should provide fertile ground for further discussion.

REFERENCES

1. American Society of Agricultural Engineers. 1985. *Erosion and soil productivity.* In Proceedings, National Symposium on Erosion and Soil Productivity. St. Joseph, Michigan.
2. Batie, Sandra S., and David E. Ervin, editors. 1985. *Farm level impacts of adopting cross-compliance programs: Policy implications.* In the Proceedings of a Symposium. Agricultural Economics Department, University of Missouri, Columbia.
3. Clark, Edwin H. II. 1985. *The off-site costs of soil erosion.* Journal of Soil and Water Conservation 40(1): 19-22.
4. Clark, Edwin H. II, Jennifer A. Haverkamp, and William Chapman. 1985. *Eroding soils: The off-farm impacts.* The Conservation Foundation, Washington, D.C.
5. Dickason, Clifford, and Daniel Piper. 1983. *Economics of agricultural erosion and sedimentation—a selected literature review.* NRE Staff Report No. AGES-830328. Economic Research Service, U.S. Department of Agriculture, Washington, D.C.
6. Doering, Otto, Andrew Schmitz, and John Miranowski. 1983. *Farm costs and exports.* In *Increasing Understanding of Public Problems and Policies—1983.* Farm Foundation, Oak Brook, Illinois.
7. Doster, D. H., D. R. Griffith, J. V. Mannering, and S. D. Parsons. 1983. *Economic returns from alternative corn and soybean tillage systems in Indiana.* Journal of Soil and Water Conservation 38(6): 504-508.
8. Governor's Soil Resources Study Commission. 1984. *Indiana's erosion and sedimentation situation.* Report of the Governor's Soil Resources Study Commission. Indianapolis, Indiana.

9. Miller, Gerald A., et al. 1982. *Soil erosion and the Iowa soil 2000 program.* Pm-1056. Cooperative Extension Service, Iowa State University, Ames.
10. Mitchell, J. K., J. C. Brach, and E. R. Swanson. 1980. *Costs and benefits of terraces for erosion control.* Journal of Soil and Water Conservation 35(5): 233-236.
11. Pierce, F. J., R. H. Dowdy, W. E. Larson, and W.A.P. Graham. 1984. *Soil productivity in the Corn Belt: An assessment of erosion's long-term effects.* Journal of Soil and Water Conservation 39(2): 131-136.
12. Rasmussen, Wayne D. 1982. *History of soil conservation, institutions and incentives.* In Harold G. Halcrow, Earl O. Heady, and Melvin L. Cotner [eds.] *Soil Conservation Policies, Institutions, and Incentives.* Soil Conservation Society of America, Ankeny, Iowa.
13. Seitz, Wesley D., C. Robert Taylor, Robert G.F. Spitze, Craig Osteen, and Mack C. Nelson. 1979. *Economic impacts of soil erosion control.* Land Economics 55(1): 28-42.
14. Soil Conservation Society of America. 1983. *Conservation tillage: A special issue.* Journal of Soil and Water Conservation 38(3).
15. Uchtmann, D. L., and W. D. Seitz. 1979. *Options for controlling nonpoint source water pollution: A legal perspective.* Natural Resources Journal 19(3): 587-609.

6

Sources of Information and Technical Assistance for Farmers in Controlling Soil Erosion

Gordon L. Bultena and Eric O. Hoiberg

History demonstrates well that reliance solely on a "technological fix" to reduce excessive soil erosion on the nation's farms is doomed to failure. Despite the longstanding availability of innovative farming practices and technologies that effectively control erosion, excessive soil loss remains one of the paramount issues in American agriculture.

With the current emphasis on voluntary approaches, control of soil erosion won't become commonplace until farmers are convinced of the need for action, persuaded by the personal benefits (economic and otherwise) of taking action, and effectively linked to institutional sources of information and financial assistance.

The onset of the "information age" has enhanced farmers' capabilities of being well informed about factors affecting their operations.[1] But even given the recent proliferation of conservation appeals and new erosion control technologies, many farmers remain oblivious to their erosion problems or indecisive about how the problems might be solved.

Information Use and the Adoption/Diffusion Model

Despite public attention to problems of soil erosion on farmland, there is a paucity of research on factors important to farmers' information-

[1]Don Dillman has explored the implications of the emergent information age for agriculture (5).

seeking behavior and conservation decision-making.[2] Several models have been formulated to help understand the role of information in farmers' decision-making. The adoption/diffusion model is the most prominent (12). A basic tenet of this model is that the information needs of farmers change as they progress through the adoption process. In other words, how information is obtained and used depends upon where farmers are in their decision-making.

In the initial stage of decision-making (awareness), farmers primarily use the mass media, especially farm magazines, for information and guidance. These media are then displaced in the evaluation and trial stages of decision-making by interpersonal networks (neighbors and friends), governmental agencies, and personal experience.

How and where farming information is obtained is viewed in the adoption/diffusion model as dependent upon adopter statuses. "Innovators," for example, bypass local information channels and draw upon more geographically remote sources deemed knowledgeable, credible, and current (e.g., university scientists). By comparison, "early adopters" are influenced most in their conservation decisions by innovators. "Later adopters," in turn, use early adopters as their primary referents for decision-making.

Information Use: What Research Has Found

There are two types of research on how conservation information is obtained and used in agriculture. First, descriptive surveys have identified the major sources of farmers' conservation information. Second, the importance of this information, versus other factors, in explaining farmers' conservation adoption behavior has been tested.

Descriptive Surveys. Considerable inquiry has been made into the sources of farmers' conservation information. Among the conclusions in this literature are that:

► Farmers often fail to perceive that they have soil erosion problems and, thus, aren't motivated to seek information and apply corrective measures.

► Farmers often overestimate the extent to which they are applying conservation practices, such as reduced tillage.

► Consistent with predictions from the adoption/diffusion model, different information sources prevail at the several stages of decision-making. Mass media are especially important during awareness, but are

[2]Everett Rogers concluded: "Compared to other aspects of diffusion research, there have been relatively few studies of how the social or communicative structure of a system affects the diffusion and adoption of innovations in that system" (12).

displaced by interpersonal sources (family, neighbors, and friends) at later stages of decision-making.

► Overall, mass media (especially farm magazines), government agencies, interpersonal contacts, and personal experiences are the most salient sources of new farming information, although many other sources are also used.

► Farmers' personal and farm-firm characteristics affect their use of information sources. Those with the largest operations and the greatest influence in local affairs, tend most often to draw upon public agencies for farming information.

► Farmers' perceptions of soil erosion are associated with their implementation of U.S. Department of Agriculture farm conservation plans.

Importance of Information Variables for Adoption Behavior. Few studies have used information as a variable to explain farmers' conservation behavior, and the evidence is mixed as to its importance.[3] A recent Ohio study (*10*) showed that use of information sources was of little importance in explaining farmers' adoption of conservation practices. This led the authors to conclude: "The study findings clearly bring into question the use of education type programs to increase the adoption of conservation tillage practices.... Reliance on an information-based program to convince farmers to adopt conservation tillage practices will probably prove futile."

Using a quasi-experimental design, Korsching and associates (*8*) recently tested the effectiveness of information dissemination for altering farmers' conservation opinions and behavior. Informative posters were placed in popular gathering places of farmers, such as cafes, hardware stores, and elevators. The posters were to increase farmers' awareness of the nature and consequences of excessive soil erosion (especially sheet erosion), encourage their acceptance of the necessity and benefits of practicing good conservation and better acquaint them with the technical and financial services available from local conservation agencies.

Impacts of the informational campaign were evaluated by testing for changes in the attitudes and conservation behavior of farmers living in control and experimental counties in western Iowa. Although post-test analysis revealed that many respondents had seen and/or discussed the informational materials, the study failed to show that these materials had any effect upon their subsequent conservation views or behavior.[4]

More positive effects of information dissemination on farmers' con-

[3]Studies of factors important to the conservation behavior of farmers are listed in Napier and Forster (*9*), Rogers (*12*), Stofferahn and Korsching (*13*), and van Es (*14*).
[4]The failure in this study to produce a more positive outcome could have resulted from the short period of time between the intervention and evaluation efforts.

servation behavior is shown in other studies (*1, 6, 7, 11*). Parent and Lovejoy, for example, found that the frequency of agency contacts among Indiana farmers was related to farmers' attendance at informational meetings, which, in turn, served to elevate their perceptions of conservation problems.[5] The role of information dissemination in boosting problem perception proved important; perception was found to be a major determinant of conservation adoptions.

An Interregional Study

In 1983 we sought to determine the extent to which farmers in erosion-prone areas throughout the United States were using alternative sources of conservation information to control soil loss. More than 3,200 farm operators were interviewed by telephone. Respondents were drawn from 13 states with comparatively high levels of soil loss (Figure 1). At the time of the study, 64 of the 112 counties involved had been targeted by the U.S. Department of Agriculture for special erosion control assistance. The remaining 48 counties were selected for study by Soil Conservation Service state conservationists on the basis that their topographic, soil, agronomic, and socioeconomic conditions were similar to those of targeted counties.

Respondents in each county were randomly selected from *Farm and Ranch Directories.* In areas where directories were unavailable, names of potential respondents were obtained by randomly sampling rural telephone directories. Respondents in the Palouse area of Washington and Idaho were randomly selected from a list of all farm operators compiled for another purpose. To be eligible for inclusion in the study, respondents had to gross $1,000 or more annually in agricultural sales.

A total of 9,178 rural households in the 13 states were contacted and screened. Of these, 3,910 households (43 percent) produced an eligible respondent, 83 percent of whom were interviewed.[6]

A Summary of Findings

The 13-state study was based on five questions:

Question 1. Are farmers sufficiently aware of, and concerned about, soil erosion to seek conservation information?

Question 2. What are the primary sources of farmers' conservation information at various stages in their decision-making? Do they use the in-

---

[5]Parent, Dale F., and Stephen B. Lovejoy. 1984. "Diffusion of Conservation Technologies: A Test of the Market and Infrastructure Perspective." Paper presented at the Rural Sociological Society meeting.

[6]A detailed description of the sample and survey procedures was reported by Bultena and associates (*3*).

formation sources that are available to them?

Question 3. What type of farmers make the greatest use of alternative information sources?

Question 4. What characteristics of information sources are important to their selection?

Question 5. What role does personal influence play in conservation decisions of farmers?

Question 1. Are farmers sufficiently aware of, and concerned about, soil erosion to seek conservation information? Research has shown that farmers often underestimate the extent and severity of their soil losses. A common tendency is to attribute more serious erosion problems to others. This phenomenon is called the "proximity effect." There was evidence in our 13-state study of a proximity effect: 92 percent of the farmers perceived soil erosion as being a problem in their home counties, 78 percent in their local communities, but only 66 percent on their own farms, despite being located in areas that rank high nationally in soil loss.

These perceptions of farmers are important to efforts by agencies to control erosion. A positive relationship existed in our study between recognition of erosion problems and the use of information sources. Farmers who perceived erosion as a problem at the county, community, and farm levels were also the most aggressive in seeking conservation information and assistance.

Although the reasons some farmers denied having personal erosion problems were not explored in the study, several explanations seem plausible. These included (1) the absence of erosion problems, (2) a desire to reduce psychological stress associated with the recognition of a problem that is going unmet, (3) the belief that soil erosion is a normal or natural phenomenon, (4) a lack of awareness of the magnitude of their personal soil losses, (5) a perception that only the most dramatic instances of erosion (e.g., gully versus sheet erosion) constitute problems, and (6) a feeling that they are already effectively dealing with erosion.

That a substantial number of farmers deny having soil erosion problems points up the continuing need by conservation agencies to publicize the often subtle nature of soil losses, as well as to raise public consciousness of what are tolerable and intolerable loss levels. Our data show that the perception of erosion problems by local farmers cannot be taken for granted, even in areas where soil losses are endemic and severe.

Question 2. What are the primary sources of farmers' conservation information at various stages in their decision-making? Do they use the information sources that are available to them? Respondents were queried about their use in 1982 of seven alternative sources of conservation information. An average of 2.5 information sources were used (the range was from zero to seven sources). Some persons (14 percent) used no sources. Half used two or fewer sources.

The most commonly used information source was "farm magazines and newspapers," mentioned by 72 percent. A smaller but sizeable number used "neighbors, friends, and relatives" (47 percent); a "selected government agency" (12 to 33 percent, depending upon the agency); and "farm product dealers" (31 percent).

Of particular interest was the use being made of institutional sources (public agencies). Nearly half (46 percent) of the respondents had no contact in 1982 with any of the four conservation agencies we studied—SCS, Agricultural Stabilization and Conservation Service, Cooperative Extension Service, and local conservation district commissioners. Twenty percent had contact with a single agency and 29 percent with two or more agencies.

The relationship between farmers' contact with government agencies and their use of noninstitutional sources (peers, mass-media, dealers) was explored as well in our study. Persons using agencies as information sources were also those who most frequently consulted peers, farm publications, and commercial dealers. Obviously, access to institutional sources does not dampen and probably stimulates farmers' propensity to seek information from informal, noninstitutional sources.

From the perspective of the adoption/diffusion model, the primary sources of farmers' information can be expected to change as they progress through the decision-making process. To explore such shifts, respondents were asked where they would go for assistance or information in four different situations, the first three of which roughly corresponded to stages in the adoption/diffusion model:

► To determine if they had a soil erosion problem.

► To find out what conservation practices might be needed on their farms.

► To find out how to use or incorporate a conservation practice into their operations.

► To ascertain the economic costs and benefits of different conservation measures.

Government agencies were the most frequently identified sources for each of the four information needs, drawing from 75 to 85 percent of all mentions. SCS was listed most often for each information need, followed by ASCS and the Cooperative Extension Service. Universities received fewer mentions for these items, but were seen by some persons (9 percent of the mentions) as a primary source of information about the economic costs and benefits of conservation practices.

The repeated mention of SCS, ASCS, and Extension as likely sources of conservation assistance suggests that these agencies enjoy substantial visibility and credibility among farm people. But despite their prominence as preferred information sources, the sobering fact remains that half of our respondents had no contact with any government conservation agency in the year preceding the survey, and 44 percent had never considered obtaining a farm conservation plan.

The conservation agencies listed as probable sources of information in some of the four areas of assistance suggest that there is considerable confusion among farmers about the missions and programs of these agencies. For example, ASCS was often seen as a primary source of assistance for identifying erosion problems and for determining needed conservation practices. Confusion about agency missions probably results from the fact that conservation assistance today is fragmented among several agencies; there is no single source to which farmers can turn for both financial and technical aid.

Several actions by conservation agencies could seemingly help to reduce farmers' confusion about where to go for different types of assistance. First, more effort should be given to informing farmers about the types of assistance that can be secured from different sources. Second, there is a need for governmental agencies to better coordinate the delivery of their conservation services. Farmers' confusion about appropriate information sources can be addressed by effective referral once persons enter the "service network." The feasibility of a referral system is indicated by our finding that a sizeble number of those who had consulted specific conservation agencies in 1982 also had contacted other agencies.

Question 3. What type of farmers make the greatest use of alternative information sources? In addition to the fact that specific information sources may predominate at different stages of farmers' decision-making, it must be recognized that farmers themselves differ considerably in their solicitation and use of conservation information. Our data show that persons who were drawing upon conservation agencies for assistance were, on the whole, younger, better educated, and farming larger operations than those without agency contacts. A related finding is that the clientele of various conservation agencies differ in some personal and farm characteristics. Average farm size, for example, was substantially larger for those reporting contacts with local conservation districts or with SCS than for those using Extension or ASCS.

The recent targeting of some counties by USDA for additional financial assistance to combat soil erosion is designed to accelerate farmers' conservation efforts. Although our data are preliminary (because of the recency of targeting), we found that farmers in the counties that were first targeted had more frequent agency contact than those in nontargeted counties. Moreover, there was greater frequency of agency-initiated versus respondent-initiated contact in targeted counties.

Question 4. What characteristics of information sources are important to their selection? Insight on this question was gained by analyzing the sources of information that respondents reported as being "most useful." Two sets of findings were produced by this analysis—the number of persons listing specific sources as most useful and the number of persons using each source who defined it as most useful.

Overall, farm publications received the greatest number of mentions as the most useful information source (listed by 27 percent of all respondents), followed by SCS (14 percent), and neighbors, friends, and relatives (14 percent). For those using a specific source, SCS led the list as most useful (mentioned by 48 percent of all SCS users), followed by farm publications (37 percent), ASCS (34 percent), and neighbors, friends, and relatives (30 percent).

Respondents' reasons for selecting a most useful information source were ascertained. For SCS, five reasons predominated (receiving 12 to 19 percent of the mentions) with the agency's accessibility (19 percent), experience (18 percent), and currency of information (17 percent) mentioned most often. For ASCS, five reasons received from 12 to 24 percent of the mentions, including currency (24 percent), accessibility (15 percent), and the fact that it was perceived as being informative (14 percent), experienced (13 percent), and unbiased (12 percent). For the Cooperative Extension Service, each of five reasons received upwards of 14 percent of all mentions. This agency most often was seen as being informative (24 percent), accessible (17 percent), current (16 percent), friendly (15 percent), and experienced (14 percent). Commercial dealers were selected as the most useful information source primarily because of their conservation information (26 percent), accessibility (20 percent), currency (18 percent), and experience (12 percent).

The reasons for selecting peers and mass media as most useful were more concentrated than for the other sources. For example, 31 percent of those selecting peers listed their experience, while another 31 percent emphasized the currency of their information. For those naming mass media, 29 percent said it was because its information was current; another 26 percent emphasized its availability.

Question 5. "What role does personal influence play in the conservation decisions of farmers?" Selection of most useful information sources was a function of the respondents' overall information-seeking profiles. Three-fifths of those making comparatively high use of both institutional and noninstitutional information sources, for example, selected an institutional source as most useful. Conversely, selection of neighbors and friends as most useful was predominately made by persons who relied solely on noninstitutional sources. The selection of farm publications as most useful was especially pronounced (mentioned by 78 percent) among persons who had made relatively little use of either institutional or non-institutional sources.

The frequent naming of family, friends, and neighbors as the most useful information source, especially by those with little or no agency contact, substantiates a finding of previous research that informal social networks perform a vital role for some in farm decision-making. The educational and promotional programs of conservation agencies have tended to overlook the importance of these informal social groups. Farmers are often seen by agencies as autonomous agents who require continuous inputs of factual information to operate rationally. But the decision about what is rational may be shaped more by the views of peers than by access to agency information. It is evident, for example, that community norms condoning excessive soil erosion have impaired agency efforts to convince persons of the need to adopt better soil conservation practices.

It seems that conservation agencies could benefit by devoting more effort to identifying and using informal support networks in their promotional and educational activities. An especially important target audience may be the "tillage clubs" emerging in many communities. More effort might also be given to disseminating information through the mass media, especially farm magazines. Use of diverse, nontraditional outlets can serve to expand the audience for conservation messages, especially among persons who in the past have proven difficult to reach and motivate to action.

Information and Education, a Complex Undertaking

Persuading farmers to adopt needed conservation practices is a complex undertaking. This complexity is demonstrated by the continued failure of many farmers to use recommended practices despite being presented with persuasive reasons for their adoption. Research on how farmers obtain and use conservation information suggests that many factors must be considered in planning information programs. For example, it is false to assume that farmers are an undifferentiated, homogeneous group, that they possess similar needs, interests, attitudes, and goals. On the contrary, there is a substantial diversity in their personal and farm-firm characteristics, their value orientations, and their preferred methods of information delivery. To be effective, change agents must recognize and deal with this diversity. To obtain successful educational outcomes will necessitate, among other things, a more refined targeting of messages to persons who display like characteristics, orientations, and conservation needs.

Research demonstrates that information needs and preferred techniques of information delivery vary considerably within the farm population. What constitutes an effective information channel or strategy for reaching one segment of farmers may prove ineffective for reaching other segments. For example, intensive information users are typically younger, have more education, operate larger farms, and are most likely to use a variety of channels to secure conservation information. In contrast, older and less educated persons and those on the smaller acreages make less use of agencies and typically prefer receiving their information from noninstitutional sources, such as peers and farm magazines. Conservation agents must identify and use multiple information channels to disseminate information and appeals. For smaller farmers, who often reside on the most marginal agricultural land, this may require a concerted effort to work through informal networks rather than to rely on the more traditional, self-initiated agency contacts.

A second false assumption is that the dissemination of information is in itself sufficient to produce meaningful attitudinal and behavioral change. Farmers often resist changing their established practices, especially when these are consistent with local norms and values. Furthermore, established farming practices, even when at cross-purposes with public goals, tend to be perceived by farmers as rational and, thus, desirable. Clearly, change agents, to be effective, must appreciate the complexity of social and psychological forces that affect how conservation messages are received and evaluated by their clientele.

Third, it is evident that, despite years of educational programming, many farmers in erosion-prone areas remain oblivious to the extent of their personal soil losses or discount the severity of these losses. This may be partly a function of their sensitivity to the more visible forms of erosion, such as gully erosion, and a lack of awareness of the more insidious forms, such as sheet and rill erosion. There must be a heightened consciousness among farmers of the long-term effects of sheet and rill erosion on the future productivity of their land and the value of that land. Also, research and educational efforts that detail off-site damages to wells and overall water quality should be developed and disseminated to farmers and the public at large. But even if all of these educational efforts are undertaken, some individuals will still staunchly resist appeals to alter their behavior.

Historically, public agencies dealing with agriculture have favored the use of the *empirical rational* strategy (4) for bringing about behavioral change among clients. This strategy, which is based on the creation of knowledge through research and its dissemination through public education, is predicated on the assumption that humans are rational and will adjust their attitudes and behavior when it is demonstrated that such changes serve their self-interests. As shown above, serious questions can be raised about the soundness of building a program of behavioral change that draws solely on the tenets of the empirical rational strategy.

An alternative but in some ways complementary strategy, the *normative reeducative* approach, rests on the assumption that human behavior is supported by social and community norms. While not completely dismissing human rationality, the normative reeducative strategy entails more than mere dissemination of technical information. Attention is also paid to attitudes, beliefs, and norms that may constitute significant barriers to public acceptance of new ideas and appeals. Of particular importance to the normative reeducative strategy are clients' informal social networks. Basic changes in values, beliefs, and norms are felt to accrue more from interaction with friends, relatives, and neighbors than from formalized relationships with change agencies. It is important to note that the dissemination of factual information continues to be a central focus of this strategy. The primary difference from the empirical rational approach is an explicit recognition that local, informal social networks constitute the most salient target in an agency's informational programming.

Historically, conservation programs have been noncoercive, depending on voluntary compliance emanating from the self-interests of clientele groups. A final strategy, the *power-coercive* approach, involves the use of political or economic sanctions to secure a target group's behavioral compliance with a predetermined change objective. The dissemination of information tends to be controlled by agencies and representatives of those in power and is used less for educational than for compliance purposes. Today, there is increasing public support for implementing mandatory programs, such as cross-compliance, where economic sanctions are used to achieve conservation goals.

In each of the above strategies, information dissemination plays a major if somewhat different role in bringing about behavioral change. Conservation officials must be aware of the alternative strategies available for securing their goals, as well as implications of the use of these strategies.

Finally, unquestioning reliance on extant models, such as the adoption-diffusion model, has produced an overly simplistic view of the dissemination and use of conservation information. The role of information in conservation decision-making is decidedly more complex today than the processes portrayed in these models. The interregional study suggests, for example, that there is not the easily identified, functional differentiation of information sources as persons move through the adoption process. Instead, multiple sources tend to be mobilized throughout the decision-making process as persons weigh the pros and cons of alternative conservation actions.

There especially is a need to direct more attention to how structural or institutional factors affect how people embrace new products and ideas (2). The conventional adoption-diffusion model fails to incorporate many potentially important determinants of farmers' conservation behavior, such as the availability and adequacy of local information and assistance networks. This is not to discount the continued use of the model, but to suggest that greater attention to other models will further enhance understanding of how farmers make and implement conservation decisions.

REFERENCES

1. Abd-Ella, Mokhtar M., Eric O. Hoiberg, and Richard Warren. 1981. *Adoption behavior in family farm systems: An Iowa study.* Rural Sociology 46(1): 42-61.
2. Brown, Lawrence A. 1981. *Innovation diffusion: A new perspective.* Methuen, New York, New York.
3. Bultena, Gordon L., Eric O. Hoiberg, and Peter J. Nowak. 1984. *Sources of conservation information and participation in conservation programs: An interregional analysis.* Sociology Report 156. Department of Sociology and Anthropology, Iowa State University, Ames.
4. Chin, Robert, and Kenneth D. Benne. 1969. *General strategies for effecting changes in human systems.* In Warren Bennis, Kenneth Benne, and Robert Chin [editors] *The Planning of Change.* Holt, Rinehart, and Winston, Inc., New York, New York. pp. 32-59.
5. Dillman, Don A. 1985. *The social impacts of information technologies in rural North America.* Rural Sociology 50(1): 1-26.
6. Ervin, David E. 1982. *Perceptions, attitudes, and risk: Overlooked variables in formulating public policy on soil conservation and water quality.* In Lee Christensen and John A. Miranowski [editors] *Perceptions, Attitudes and Risk: Overlooked Variables in Formulating Public Policy on Soil Conservation and Water Quality.* ERS Staff Report No. AGES820129. Economic Research Service, U.S. Department of Agriculture, Washington, D.C.
7. Korsching, Peter F. 1984. *Farm operation characteristics, institutional support, and the use of soil and water conservation technologies.* Southern Rural Sociology 2: 43-57.
8. Korsching, Peter F., Thomas J. Hoban, and Jane Maestro-Scherer. 1985. *The selling of soil conservation: A test of the voluntary approach. Volume I. Farmer survey.* Sociology Report 157. Department of Sociology and Anthropology, Iowa State University, Ames.
9. Napier, Ted L., and D. Lynn Forster. 1982. *Farmer attitudes and behavior associated with soil erosion control.* In Harold G. Halcrow, Earl O. Heady, and Melvin L. Cotner [editors] *Soil Conservation Policies, Institutions and Incentives.* Soil Conservation Society of America, Ankeny, Iowa. pp. 137-150.
10. Napier, Ted L., Cameron S. Thraen, Akia Gore, and W. Richard Goe. 1984. *Factors affecting the adoption of conventional and soil conservation tillage practices in Ohio.* Journal of Soil and Water Conservation 39(3): 205-209.
11. Nowak, Peter J., and Peter F. Korsching. 1983. *Social and institutional factors affecting the adoption and maintenance of agricultural BMPs.* In F. Schaller and G. Bailey [editors] *Agricultural Management and Water Quality.* Iowa State University Press, Ames.
12. Rogers, Everett M. 1983. *Diffusion of innovations.* The Free Press, New York, New York.
13. Stofferahn, Curtis W., and Peter F. Korsching. 1980. *Communication, diffusion and adoption of innovations: A bibliographical update.* Public Administration Series Bibliography No. p-433. Vance Bibliographies, Monticello, Illinois.
14. van Es, J. C. 1985. *Bibliography of socioeconomic research on the adoption and diffusion of soil and water conservation practices.* Department of Agricultural Economics., University of Illinois, Champaign.

7

Early Adopters and Nonusers of No-till in the Pacific Northwest: A Comparison

John E. Carlson and Don A. Dillman

No-till farming is relatively new in the Palouse region of eastern Washington and northern Idaho. The first no-till drill was made by a local farmer and used initially in 1974. Since then the use of such drills has increased slowly. About 25 percent of the farmers in the region had at least tried the practice by early 1985.

No-till drills developed before the mid-1970s were unsuitable for the Palouse because of the region's heavy loess soils and steep hillsides. These land characteristics require heavier, stronger no-till drills than those that were commercially available before that time. The new no-till drills are also expensive, ranging from $30,000 to $175,000.

The Palouse is recognized as one of the regions in the United States with a critical soil erosion problem. Cultivated slopes are exceptionally steep, averaging 15 to 20 percent and sometimes approaching 50 percent. Despite severe erosion, the deep loess soils continue to be highly productive. Rainfall averages 14 inches a year in the western part of the region; it increases to 26 inches some 50 miles to the east where the Palouse hills meet the foothills of the Bitterroot Range of the Rocky Mountains.

Rain falls gently and almost exclusively in winter and early spring, giving erosion a subtle character. This contrasts with conditions in the Midwest, where torrential spring downpours cause dramatic soil loss. Although deep rills and gullies appear in early spring on Palouse slopes, all traces of erosion are usually eliminated by one trip across a field with normal cultivation equipment. Large gullies and sheet erosion resulting from rainfall on frozen ground cause frequent concern, but their occa-

83

sional nature hides the continuing, substantial losses of soil. It is probably for these reasons that erosion control has progressed somewhat slowly in the Palouse.

A variety of erosion control practices are currently used in the region. These include seeding on the contour, seeding critical areas to grass, divided slopes, elimination of summer fallow, crop residue mulching, leaving stubble standing during the winter, and minimum tillage. No-till is among the most effective soil erosion control practices available.

A Recent Innovation

No-till in the Palouse remains in the early stages of adoption. In this sense, all who have used no-till are considered innovators and early adopters. Based on past adoption research, the characteristics of these farmers should differ significantly from farmers who have never used no-till. Research suggests that innovators are venturesome, take risks, have higher levels of education, make more money, and operate larger farms. They travel widely to seek out information, rely less on their neighbors for information, and worry less about what their neighbors think. They are likely to be younger, and often they farm with relatives (*1*).

Most research has looked at adopters of an innovation after the innovation has been accepted widely. Comparisons are then made of those who adopted the innovation early with those who adopted it later. A major problem with this type of analysis is the possible memory bias due to the long period since the early adopters first used the innovation. Information networks may be difficult to reconstruct 15 to 20 years after a person has used a product. In some cases the innovator may no longer be using the innovation under study; he or she may instead be using a newer version or even have substituted a different innovation for the original one.

The analysis reported here is based on interviews conducted 11 years after the first use of no-till. Even less time had elapsed since a majority of users started using the practice. Knowing that the typical random sample nets only a few of the earliest adopters, we sought to interview all farmers known to have used no-till. This allowed us to divide our sample according to time of adoption and to trace the social networks that emerged during the early stages of the adoption process. Problems of recall were minimized because of the early stage of no-till adoption.

Our objective was to compare all innovators and early adopters of no-till farming with a random sample of nonusers of no-till on the basis of their socioeconomic backgrounds, perceptions of the soil erosion problem, perceptions of no-till, and sources of information about no-till.

The Farmer Survey

To identify all farmers in the Palouse who had used no-till, lists were constructed with the help of Soil Conservation Service (SCS) offices in Whitman County, Washington, and Latah County, Idaho. A control sample was drawn randomly from lists of all farm operators obtained from the Agricultural Stabilization and Conservation Service offices in these counties. Farmers who were using no-till were removed from the control group.

Interviewing began in November 1984 and was completed by late March 1985. Of the 187 no-till farmers, 174 interviews were completed, a 93 percent response rate. Of the 140 eligible farmers in the control group, 114 interviews were completed, an 81 percent response rate.

The interview schedule was constructed with the assistance of SCS personnel. It was based in part on detailed, unstructured interviews with 12 of the earliest no-till users in the Palouse who had been interviewed the preceding year and on ethnographic observations at many no-till seminars and tours. The 12 early interviews, which were taped and later transcribed, provided essential information about the use of no-till and its early development. The formal interview schedule used much of this information. The information was then pretested on several no-till farmers outside the sample area. Identical questions were asked of both the no-till farmers and control-group farmers to the extent possible.

The Survey Results: A Comparison

Socioeconomic Characteristics. No-till users differed significantly from nonusers on certain socioeconomic characteristics. No-till users tended to be somewhat younger or older than the random sample. More important perhaps, they farmed more land, especially rented land; had higher incomes; and had more education. They also were more likely to farm under a family corporation. These findings, for the most part, confirmed that no-till innovators in the Palouse were similar socioeconomically to innovators identified in previous research.

Perceptions About Soil Erosion. As mentioned, no-till is among the most effective soil erosion control practices available to farmers in the Palouse. Therefore, users of no-till might be expected to be more aware of soil erosion than nonusers. Both samples were asked a series of questions relating to soil erosion to determine if such differences existed.

No-till users were slightly more likely to agree that "I am doing about everything I can reasonably do to control soil erosion on my farm" (Table 1). This statement produced the greatest agreement between the two groups, and it was the only statement that no-till users were more likely to agree with.

Greatest differences occurred in the case of the following two statements: "Unless soil erosion is controlled to a greater extent than it presently is, yields will decrease quite a bit in the next 10 to 20 years," and "Some form of regulation is necessary to adequately control soil erosion in the Palouse area." Less agreement by no-till users with these statements may indicate that users of no-till felt no-till was the solution to soil erosion without lower yields or the need for outside regulation. This notion was reinforced by the fact that no-till users were more likely to indicate that they were using all or most of the available soil erosion control practices.

There were no great differences between the two groups with regard to perceptions about soil erosion. But the responses suggested that no-till users may have a broader perspective of the soil erosion problem than nonusers. Users tended to perceive the indirect impacts of erosion as more serious than nonusers. Differences were greatest for the areas of

Table 1. Agreement with statements about soil erosion by no-till users and nonusers.

Statement	Percentage Agreeing with Statement	
	No-till Users	Nonusers
I am doing about everything I can reasonably do to control soil erosion on my farm	84 (33)*	80 (26)
Unless soil erosion is controlled to a greater extent than it presently is, yields will decrease quite a bit in the next 10 to 20 years	56 (14)	64 (10)
If I were to do more than I now do to control soil erosion, my yields would go down quite a bit	30 (5)	34 (2)
Some form of regulation is necessary to adequately control soil erosion in the Palouse area	23 (3)	32 (5)
Most farmers in the Palouse area aren't very concerned about soil erosion on their farms	8 (0)	10 (2)
Very little can be done about controlling soil erosion in this area because of weather and topography	7 (1)	14 (2)
Soil erosion is something we don't need to worry about because it doesn't have much effect on our yields	0 (0)	3 (1)

*Numbers in parentheses indicate percentage strongly agreeing with the statement.

Table 2. Effect of no-till on income per acre for no-till users and nonusers.

No-till Results	No-till Users		Nonusers	
	N	%	N	%
Substantially more income/acre	4	2	0	0
Somewhat more income/acre	34	20	5	4
About the same income/acre	57	33	22	19
Somewhat less income/acre	38	22	48	42
Substantially less income/acre	38	22	19	17
Don't know	1	10	20	18
Total	172	100	114	100

"downstream siltation," "long-run production and profit decreases," and "siltation of roadside ditches." No difference existed with regard to seriousness of "loss of topsoil" and "water pollution." Nonusers were much more likely to view "fouling of livestock water" as a serious problem. Nonusers may have been more involved with livestock in their farm operations.

With one exception, only minor differences emerged between no-till users and nonusers on the importance of selected practices in controlling soil erosion. No-till users were more likely to indicate that "elimination of summer fallow" was very important (59 percent compared to 39 percent indicated very important). This difference likely related to the connection between no-till and moisture retention. Summer fallow is used in the Palouse primarily for moisture retention, but it is also viewed by most farmers as a primary cause of soil erosion. No-till is known to hold more moisture in the ground than conventional tillage and to be effective in controlling soil erosion. No-till users likely would view elimination of summer fallow as an important factor in controlling soil erosion in the Palouse. No other differences exceeded 7 percent, and most were within a couple of percentage points.

Perceptions About No-Till. No-till users were asked a series of questions about their experiences with no-till. Nonusers were asked the same questions about no-till from the perspective of how they perceived no-till on the basis of what they had read, seen, or heard about the practice.

Table 2 compares no-till users and nonusers with regard to their perceptions of how no-till and conventional farming affected net income per acre. No-till users were more likely to indicate that no-till resulted in more net income per acre than conventional tillage (22 percent compared to 4 percent).

Minor differences in perception between no-till users and nonusers emerged with regard to inputs of fuel, farm labor, time spent in the field, and amount of seed. More than 72 percent of both groups felt that the same or less of each of these inputs would be used. With regard to herbicides, fertilizer, and insecticides, however, nonusers consistently felt that more of each would be necessary in no-till farming. Users of no-till were more likely to indicate that the same amount or less of these inputs were used in no-till than in conventional tillage.

Motivations for Using No-Till. Motivation among farmers for using no-till was determined by asking how important each of a series of issues would be in deciding whether or not to use no-till. Erosion control, moisture retention, and improving net farm income were the most important reasons indicated by both users and nonusers (Table 3). Substantial differences between the two groups occurred on several items. Users were more likely to try no-till because they were experimenting with a new farming technique. This is characteristic of innovators and early adopters. Reducing fuel usage and farm labor, weed control, soil compaction, and the prospect of annual cropping were more likely to be important reasons for nonusers to try no-till.

The Future of No-Till. No-till users gave no-till a more favorable prognosis for future use on their own land than did nonusers. Sixty-three percent of the no-till users compared to 38 percent of the nonusers indicated that they would probably use no-till in the future. The most common reasons given for use of no-till in the future were soil erosion con-

Table 3. *Reasons for deciding to use no-till for no-till users and nonusers.*

Reason	Percentage Indicating "Somewhat" or "Very" Important Reason	
	No-till Users	Nonusers
	%	
Erosion control	97 (86)*	94 (84)
Moisture retention	86 (51)	88 (51)
Improving net farm income	84 (44)	89 (61)
An interesting experiment with a new farming technique	79 (29)	67 (18)
Reducing time spent in field	77 (26)	79 (29)
Reducing fuel consumption	73 (21)	87 (31)
Reducing need for farm labor	57 (13)	64 (17)
Weed control	54 (27)	85 (67)
Soil compaction	53 (16)	79 (31)
Enables annual cropping	37 (16)	58 (19)

*Number in parentheses is the percentage indicating "very" important reason.

Table 4. Sources of information about no-till.

Information Source	Percentage Receiving Information	
	No-till Users	Nonusers
Another farmer in county	81	90
Soil Conservation Service	80	93
Farm magazines or journals	71	95
Tour of no-till fields	49	62
County Extension office	40	73
Chemical dealer(s)	38	57
Directly from Washington State University/		
University of Idaho	35	59
Conference or seminar	34	47
Farm product show	28	64
Machinery dealer(s)	21	38
Farmer who lives somewhere outside of		
the county	8	22
Northwest No-till Association	5	8
Bank or other credit source	1	4

trol and reduced costs. Those undecided about future use gave cost of equipment and weed control as the most common reasons for remaining undecided. Those who did not plan to use no-till in the future gave weed control and higher expenses as the most frequent reasons for not planning to use the practice.

No-till users were more likely to indicate that they would be using no-till on a larger portion of their land three years hence than were nonusers. Little difference emerged between owned and rented land. Seventy-seven percent of the no-till users, compared to 70 percent of the nonusers, indicated that no-till use would increase in the Palouse over the next 10 years. The chief difference occurred in the "increase greatly" category; 16 percent of the users and 9 percent of the nonusers fell in this category.

Information Sources and Their Importance

Information channels are important in the adoption process. Different sources of information become important at different stages of adoption. Our survey allowed us to focus on the early adopters from the standpoint of their information networks.

Users were more likely to make telephone calls of 100 miles or more for information about no-till than were nonusers. Users were not any more likely to make calls of more than 100 miles, however. Similar results were found when asking how often respondents traveled to Spokane for any reason and to Spokane or further for farm information. No differences emerged in terms of general travel to Spokane or further but no-till users were more likely to travel to Spokane or further to seek out ideas related to their farm operations. Spokane was chosen as a reference point because it is the largest metropolitan area in the Palouse. No-till users were much more likely than nonusers to have traveled to see no-till demonstrations or to have written or talked on the telephone with someone about no-till outside the Palouse.

Both samples were asked if they received information about no-till from a number of sources and if these sources had influenced them to use or not use no-till. They were also asked to pick the source that was of greatest influence if they were a user or the greatest influence on their present attitude about no-till if they were a nonuser. In all cases a greater percentage of nonusers had received information about no-till from all sources (Table 4). This was not surprising because the question asked of no-till users focused on their source of information prior to their use of no-till, and since that time more information had become available from most sources. Nonusers responded to the question on the basis of their present sources of information.

Users were influenced to use no-till by a number of information sources (Table 5). Other farmers in the area, SCS personnel, farm magazines, chemical dealers, conferences and/or seminars, and tours of no-till fields were of greater influence to users compared with nonusers. Farm product shows, the county Extension office, and the two state universi-

Table 5. Sources of positive influence to use no-till as perceived by no-till users and nonusers.

Source of Influence	Percentage Indicating Influence to Use	
	No-till Users	Nonusers
Soil Conservation Service	60	44
Another farmer in county	60	22
Farm magazines or journals	37	32
Tour of no-till fields	37	23
Conference or seminar	24	21
Chemical dealer(s)	17	15
Directly from Washington State University/ University of Idaho	19	25
County Extension office	18	53
Farm product show	14	24
Machinery dealer(s)	12	11
Farmer who lives somewhere outside of the county	6	-
Northwest No-till Association	3	4
Bank or other credit source	-	1

ties were more likely to be sources of positive influence among nonusers. SCS was the most important influence for no-till users, while other farmers in the Palouse were the most important influence on the nonuser's current attitude toward no-till. The order was reversed for the second most important influence, and tours of no-till fields was the third most important influence for both groups.

Some Implications

It would be a mistake for promoters of no-till to assume that the no-till is being accepted by farmers mainly because of its conservation implications. Early users of no-till in the Palouse reported adopting it and continuing to use it more for its economic appeal than for its conservation benefits. Attitudes about soil conservation did not separate users from nonusers.

Judging from the large operations of those farmers using no-till and the likelihood they reported for continued use, no-till is seen as a way of farming more land efficiently. The possibility of shifting from fallow to annual cropping may be a particularly important goal for some farmers, which leads to their experimentation with no-till.

No-till does not appear to be a temporary innovation that will disappear when the novelty of the practice wears off. The fact that nearly two-thirds of the no-till users and a surprising 40 percent of the nonusers expected to be using no-till in the future suggests that its use will increase. No-till is a practice that farmers are taking seriously and attempting to integrate effectively into their farming operations on a long-term basis.

Promotional efforts for no-till are beyond the stage of creating awareness or learning the fundamentals of how it's done. Virtually every farmer knows about no-till and has had an opportunity to see how it works. The kind of promotional effort needed now is to show precisely how no-till works in specific situations. Also, previous users must be shown how to take advantage of new developments in technology that will allow them to overcome past problems, including inappropriate use of herbicides and the lack of fertilizer placement technology.

One important need with respect to no-till use in the Palouse remains: scientists and promoters of no-till must facilitate a two-way flow of information between farmers and themselves. No-till was a farmer innovation. Its use has been greatly enhanced by both public and private research. The experiences of farmers as they attempt to use no-till in new ways provide a natural laboratory for learning the potential of no-till, and these experiences will help to develop recommendations for more effective no-till use by more farmers. No-till drills and the situations in which they are used are quite different than they were only five years ago. No-till methods used in 1990 no doubt will be different than those in use today. No-till is not a static innovation, but an evolving technology.

REFERENCE

1. Carlson, John E., and Don A. Dillman. 1983. *Influence of kinship arrangement on farmer innovativeness.* Rural Sociology 48: 183-200.

III

Constraints
to Conservation

8

Constraints to Practicing Soil Conservation: Land Tenure Relationships

David E. Ervin

Farmland tenancy in the United States experienced at least three important changes during the 1970s: (1) The percentage of total farmland owned by landlords, particularly nonoperator landlords, rose; (2) use of fixed-cash rental contracts increased; and (3) landlords contributed a lesser share of total farm production and capital expenditures (*2*). Together, these events imply increased separation of ownership from management of farmland. Whether these trends will continue, change somewhat, or reverse during the current agricultural production adjustment process is unknown.

Farmland leasing has always been an integral part of the nation's agricultural industry. And soil erosion control on rented land generally is perceived as more problematic than on comparable farmland operated by its owner. However, traditional public soil conservation programs have not been designed or implemented with specific, identifiable strategies to deal with erosion control on rented farmland.

The changes in farmland tenancy, coupled with concern about erosion control on rented farmland, are surely enough to justify a special focus on the relationship between land tenure and soil conservation. Not that this subject has been ignored in the literature. On the contrary, numerous authors have addressed it. Bunce, in the early 1940s, explored the theoretical reasons for problems in achieving soil conservation on rented land (*6*). Held and Clawson reviewed several empirical studies in their comprehensive analysis of soil conservation in the early 1960s (*14*). Lee (*16*), Baron (*3*), and others (*5, 13*) have written on the subject in the 1980s with the aid of the 1977 National Resources Inventory data.

Despite these research efforts, the question of whether rented land receives less, the same, or more erosion control than owner-operated land remains an enigma. Little evidence has been produced to support or refute any of the three possible outcomes because of the difficulty in constructing rigorous tests.

The Land Tenure and Soil Conservation Relationship

Consider the following statement: A landlord-tenant combination has the same incentive to practice erosion control as an owner-operator. One can demonstrate this proposition rigorously in theory (*12*).[1] But the introduction of real-world farmland tenancy arrangements causes uncertainty about the direction and strength of the incentives for soil erosion control on rented versus owner-operated land.

In his classic work on resource conservation, Wantrup identified three potential factors associated with tenancy that may hamper the level of conservation achieved (*21*). First, he notes, instability of tenancy causes greater uncertainty, which may reduce individual and/or joint incentives for conservation. "A tenant who doubts whether his lease will be renewed will find it profitable to mine his soil, although soil conservation practices may be quite economical under more stable tenure" (*21*). This effect pertains mainly to the tenant. Landlords will continue to own the land through lease changes. They will, therefore, have an enduring incentive to invest in soil erosion control, other things being equal.

The second factor, and perhaps the most important, relates to the incidence of revenues and costs associated with conservation actions. Wantrup explains, "If all expected revenues and costs functionally related to the actions of a tenant were incident on him, he would have no reason to alter the utilization plan because of the fact that he is not the owner. In theory, the utilization plan would be the same even under short leases as under ownership" (*21*). At fault is the absence of lease provisions that properly allocate conservation benefits and costs to the landlord and tenant.

Fixed, regressive rents are mentioned as the third tenancy factor affecting conservation. Wantrup argues, "...demand for small properties by prospective tenants is greater relative to potentialities of money income than the demand for large properties" (*21*). These higher rents for lower income tenants increase their time-preference (discount) rates and result in less conservation. Whether this phenomenon is widespread to-

---

[1] An important assumption in this analysis is that of negligible or nonexistent transaction costs between landlord and tenant. If those costs are large, the likelihood of the landlord-tenant combination achieving the same level of soil erosion control as an owner-operator declines.

day is a question for empirical research.

In summary, the decision to undertake erosion control is generally different for a landlord-tenant team than for an owner-operator because of common tenancy arrangements. Assuming profit maximization as an economic goal, the owner-operator considers the effect of soil conservation on net returns while he expects to own the land. He or she also takes into account the impact of soil conservation on the land's terminal value or sale price. Only one party makes decisions about soil erosion control actions.

Matters are generally more complicated in the case of rented land. Acting in isolation, the tenant's only incentive is to invest in soil erosion control if the productivity benefits or input cost savings outweigh erosion control expenses during the time he expects to rent the land. How great this incentive is depends on the stability and length of tenure. Because the tenant does not own the land, any effect on the land's sale price is ignored unless the lease incorporates compensation.

Similarly, landlords acting on their own may underinvest in soil erosion control because some benefits will be captured by their tenants who do not share in the costs. Unless leasing arrangements incorporate a sharing of erosion control costs in proportion to benefits received, the landlord-tenant combination presumably will not pursue soil conservation to the extent that owner-operators in comparable situations will.

There may, of course, be systematic differences between owner-operator and landlord or tenant characteristics that also affect soil erosion control. Although their origin is not in tenancy arrangements, these factors may help account for a perceived difference in soil conservation on rented versus owner-operated farmland.

First, landlords may be less likely to pursue soil erosion control and leases that promote it if they lack information about the effects of erosion control on farm operations. Baron's data suggest an increasing role of nonoperator landlords unfamiliar with farm operations (2).

Second, landlords as a group may be older than owner-operators. Thus, they may possess higher discount rates that make long-term conservation investments less attractive.

A final factor not usually discussed in the theoretical literature but receiving much current comment is cash flow pressure. The argument usually proceeds as follows: extreme short-run cash flow pressure (1) forces an owner-operator, tenant, or landlord to plant the most profitable short-run crop rotation, which generally lacks forage and causes more erosion, and/or (2) does not allow the operator or owner to invest in profitable conservation practices because of the need to meet existing debt service requirements. These arguments may have some validity if many retired landlords on fixed incomes require a rising cash flow during inflationary periods and if a lot of tenants are beginning or expanding operators with high debt-equity ratios.

Both the nontenure-related factors and tenure considerations represent only potential problems that may reduce incentives for erosion control on rented versus owner-operated land. Whether they are significant factors in the soil conservation decision process only research can determine over time.

Erosion Control and Land Tenure: What Evidence?

Early research on the effect of tenure on soil erosion control seemingly supported the conventional wisdom that tenancy is associated with lower erosion control. Held and Clawson, in a review of a number of these studies, concluded that tenancy did indeed hamper soil conservation efforts (14). But the evidence they reviewed is far from convincing to the skeptical eye. Many of the efforts were case studies, the findings of which were difficult to generalize.

One careful test was conducted as a four-state, cooperative effort in the late 1950s (15). Surveys of a random sample of operators in Iowa, Missouri, Nebraska, and Kansas were conducted to test the effect of tenure arrangements on use of farm resources. Findings did not reveal significant differences in the level of investment in terraces, waterways, legumes, and pasture improvements between owner-operated and tenant-operated farms. Intrasample variation in farm erosion potential was not strictly controlled, however; so this evidence can be judged inconclusive.

Many recent research efforts have taken advantage of larger and more detailed data sets. Using 1977 NRI data and the U.S. Department of Agriculture's Economic Research Service Land Ownership Survey, Lee concluded that significant differences in soil erosion rates between tenure categories did not exist for the nation or for most regions (16). But this test relied on dividing the NRI observations into tenure classes (full owners, part owner-operators, and full tenants), which cannot yield a clear test of soil erosion control on owner-operated versus rented land (5).

Using a geographical subset of the NRI-Land Ownership Survey data base, Baron found that part or full owner-operators were more likely than nonoperating owners to invest in terraces, grass waterways, or gully control (3). Expenditures for nonstructural conservation practices, such as conservation tillage, were not considered.

Gertel and associates extended Baron's analysis by examining the frequency of capital expenditures for conservation, land clearing, and drainage by more detailed landowner groups and for the entire nation (13). The researchers found again that a significantly higher proportion of farm owner-operators reported such expenditures in 1975-1977 than nonoperating owners. Moreover, their results showed that retired nonoperator owners made these capital expenditures less often than other nonoperator owners. Neither Lee (*16*), Baron (*3*), or Gertel and associates (*13*) accounted for possible systematic variation in soil erosion potential among landowner classes.

The latest national evidence comes again from the 1977 NRI-Land Ownership Survey data base. Bills estimated that conservation management on rented land did not differ significantly from conservation management on land operated by its owner (*5*). This analysis of owner-operated versus rented land avoids the use of tenure classes and the resulting ambiguity in Lee's findings (*16*). The procedure for defining whether an NRI sample point was owner-operated or tenant-operated caused the elimination of some sample observations. Measurement of conservation management by the cover and supporting practices factors in the universal soil loss equation appears also to omit the possible differential existence of terraces between land tenure categories because terraces shorten slope length and can affect the slope steepness factors. Given his findings, Bills suggests there is no need to treat leased cropland differently than owner-operated cropland in designing soil conservation policy.

On a much smaller geographic scale, I compared the erosion control performances of a random sample of northern Missouri farmers (*11*). My findings suggested that the average soil loss rate on rented cropland was significantly greater than that on owner-operator cropland, but there was wide variation within each group. Furthermore, the higher average soil loss rate was generated on rented cropland with a lower average erodibility potential than owner-operated cropland. An analysis of variables affecting soil loss rates on rented cropland identified the presence of lease cost-sharing provisions for conservation expenses as the only significant factor. If such lease cost-sharing provisions reflect joint landlord-tenant decisions to apportion soil erosion control costs and benefits, this finding supports the importance of how such benefits and costs are dispersed among the parties.

Norris recently tested the influence of land tenure on soil erosion control with random sample data from a small Virginia area (*18*). In that study a farm operator's annual soil conservation expenditure, excluding conservation tillage costs, related negatively and significantly to the proportion of rented land in the operator's farmland base. This test is significant in that it simultaneously accounted for variation in farmland erosion potential and personal and farm factors. A critical question is whether findings in the Missouri and Virginia studies extend to a broader geographic scope.

How to Interpret the Evidence

Research findings amply portray the empirical ambiguity surrounding the influence of tenancy on soil erosion control. But a moment's reflec-

tion may help explain why these disparate results occurred. Theoretical-
ly, the primary tenure factors hampering soil erosion control on rented
land included the insecurity of tenure and the incidence of soil erosion
control costs and benefits between landlord and tenant. Systematic differences in nontenure factors between the landlord-tenant group and
owner-operators, such as age, were cited as other possible causes of less
perceived soil conservation on rented lands. But these are only *potential*
factors that impinge on *some* cropland rental situations and not on
others. Undoubtedly, there are landlord-tenant relationships that do not
suffer any of these constraints. For example, a landlord and tenant may
work under a secure lease arrangement that properly allocates benefits
and costs of soil conservation to each of the participants. In those cases,
soil erosion control should approach levels achieved by owner-operators,
other things being equal.

Empirical research, especially recent studies (*3, 5, 11, 13, 16*), has attempted to test the effect of tenure on soil erosion control by comparing
aggregate conservation performance between tenure classes or on owner-
operated versus rented land. Tests of this nature necessarily lump all
rental situations together versus all owner-operator cases. As a result, the
tests describe *average* erosion control relationships between tenure categories. In fact, there exists wide variation in erosion control conditions
within each category (*5, 11*).

Moreover, the tests generally have not controlled for other factors that
may influence soil erosion control aside from tenure, such as farm size.
This is mainly because of data limitations. Only Norris accounted for
some nontenure influences (*18*). Ervin and Ervin, who proposed a
theoretical model of soil conservation decisions incorporating physical,
personal, economic, and institutional influences, found empirical support for a variety of influences (*9*). This line of reasoning suggests that it
is impossible to test rigorously the relationship between land tenure and
soil erosion control without simultaneously controlling tenure conditions
and other important factors influencing soil conservation decisions.

Erosion Control Strategies for Rented Farmland

Even if one accepts findings that no significant differences exist in
average conservation performance between rented and owner-operated
land, does it follow that soil conservation programs for the two types of
land need not be differentiated?[2] I suggest not. Certain owner-operators
have soil erosion control problems. And certain types of land tenancy

---

[2]Bills' argument that public soil erosion control efforts need not be differentiated between leased cropland and owner-operator cropland may refer to general soil conservation
policy development rather than program implementation or the nature of conservation
assistance programs for each category (*5*).

situations have soil erosion control problems. But the approaches to providing public assistance, that is, program implementation, must recognize the inherently different decision processes of owner-operators and landlord-tenant combinations. Both theoretical and empirical research clearly demonstrate the different influences in each process.

A series of steps can be used to describe the logical sequence of activities in a program implementation strategy for rented land:

A. Study the local/regional farmland rental market. Local custom and tradition play an important role in determining common tenancy arrangements (*21*). It is critical, therefore, that public conservation agencies first understand the nature of those common tenancy arrangements. Several questions must be considered:

1. Are cropland leases generally informal, unwritten arrangements or more formal written agreements?

2. Are cropland leases normally crop-share or cash, or some combination, and what types of landlords and tenants use each?

3. How are production and conservation expenses shared in the different types of leases, if at all?

4. What lengths are most common for the different lease types?

5. Do leases commonly include provision for notification of each party a sufficient time before expiration?

6. What conditions must be met for renewal?

7. Are there provisions in the leases to compensate owners for damages by tenants?

8. Are there provisions to compensate tenants for unexhausted improvements that they have made to the cropland upon lease expiration?

Answers to these questions will provide public conservation personnel with a working knowledge of the local and regional farmland rental market. That knowledge will prove helpful in recommendations to landlords or tenants for overcoming possible soil erosion control problems on rented land.

B. Determine what type of landlord-tenant situations exist. The next step is to identify which landlord-tenant combinations may require assistance to achieve more soil erosion control. A typology of rental situations will help identify rental circumstances that may deserve priority. There may be other tenancy conditions, of course, and the following categories are not necessarily mutually exclusive.

1. *Intra-family lease.* There seems to be little cause for concern when one family member rents land from another, especially father and son. Carlson and Dillman, in a study of Palouse farmers, found that farming arrangements between relatives, which imply an eventual intergenerational transfer of property, have a positive effect on soil conservation in-

novation (7). This type of lease relationship should provide little problem for soil erosion control unless factors unrelated to tenure, for example, cash flow, prove to be significant constraints.

2. *Prospective owner lease.* Bills noted correctly that when tenants have longer term ownership motives they are more likely to care for the land as if they own it (5). Only restrictive lease conditions that do not allow the equitable sharing of conservation benefits and costs or regressive rents might hamper the economically profitable control of erosion.

3. *Operator-operator lease.* If the landlord is also an operator, there is a greater likelihood that he or she will recognize the potential costs and benefits of soil erosion control. But for one of many reasons (e.g., personal preference, community customs), the lease may not be designed to aid erosion control actions that could provide net benefits to both parties. Still, this rental situation should provide fewer soil conservation problems than the nonoperating owner category.

4. *Nonoperating owner.* Although there is no empirical measure to cite, I suspect that most concern with soil erosion control on rented land applies to nonfamily landlords who are not operators and have tenants who do not intend to purchase the land. There are several dimensions to this category that define the following subgroups: (a) former operator versus no operating experience, (b) widow or child of former operator, (c) individual and family owners versus nonfamily partnerships and corporations, (d) retired versus not retired, and (e) local versus absentee.

Logic suggests that former operators should have a greater familiarity with erosion control costs and benefits than owners with no farm experience. To a lesser extent, this probably also applies to widows and children of former operators. Soil conservation obstacles in cases where the owner has little or no operating experience would come most likely from the absence of acceptable cost-benefit sharing provisions for conservation or nontenure factors, such as age or cash-flow pressure.

Some might argue that nonoperating owners, whether individuals or families, might be more likely to invest in conservation than nonfamily partnerships and corporations. Gertel and associates could not support this hypothesis in their analysis (13). However, nonoperating individuals and families as well as nonfamily, nonoperator partnerships and corporations invested in conservation significantly fewer times than owner-operators.

Another frequent villian in the conservation debate is the absentee landlord. Studies to date, however, do not show that owners living outside the county[3] where the rented land is located fall below their local

---

[3]One weakness of research on absentee landlords' conservation attitudes and behavior is the need to define absentee with reference to residence outside the county or distance from the rented land. While distance is a relevant parameter, it is a less-than-perfect predictor of the landlord's involvement in farming operations.

counterparts (*8, 13*). Data from a northern Missouri county provide one clue why absentee landlord's soil erosion control efforts may be perceived as insufficient (*10*). In that study, the sample cropland's erodibility and whether the landlord was absentee correlated directly and significantly. In other words, absentee owners more likely possessed more erodible land.

Finally, there may be a need to distinguish between retired nonoperating owners and those who are not retired. Economic reasoning suggests that as age increases the value landowners place on distant conservation benefits will decline. As a result, they are less likely to take erosion control action than younger owners. Gertel and associates found that retired, nonoperating landlords, as a group, were significantly less likely to have undertaken conservation capital expenditures than nonoperating landlords who were not retired (*13*). This argument has nothing directly to do with land tenure per se, except that the age distribution of nonoperating landlords is probably greater than that of owner-operators.

C. Develop program elements to suit particular land tenancy-related conservation problems. The final step in implementing soil conservation programs on rented cropland is to match program efforts with the source of constraints on erosion control identified for each rental situation. As argued, some of these constraints are tenure-related. Others stem from systematic differences in landlord and owner-operator characteristics (e.g., age).

A first issue is whether to focus on the landlord or tenant or both. Traditional erosion control assistance programs most often aim at operators. Current operators are more likely to perceive the immediate benefits of conservation. But unless tenant operators expect to rent the land for an extended period of time or intend to purchase the land, a program oriented to renters will miss the long-term incentives that owners have. Barkley argued that the landowner has more incentive to maintain his or her soil stock to preserve wealth (*1*). Moreover, landowners generally have greater control over leasing provisions. Erosion control programs on rented land thus should be aimed primarily at landowners. But the following erosion control program for rented land contains elements for both parties:[4]

1. *Legislative review.* Prior to developing educational programs and model lease recommendations, soil conservation agencies in each state should review possible lease contractual relationships for adequacy. This review should include the following: (a) landlord and tenant rights to termination notice, (b) allowable lease lengths, (c) compulsory arbitration

[4]Parts of this program for erosion control on rented cropland were outlined in a previous paper (*10*).

of disputes, and (d) rights to compensation for unexhausted improvements and damages (6). These elements provide the necessary legal framework for tenure security and the proper sharing of erosion control costs and benefits.

2. *Educational component.* Based on the premise that public soil conservation programs should help alleviate constraints to owners or operators adopting socially profitable practices, a first step is to fully educate both parties about private erosion control costs and benefits. In other words, soil conservation programs should not attempt to persuade landowners or tenants to use socially unprofitable practices. Without some understanding of private costs and benefits, neither party will accurately perceive the incentives associated with conservation.

Two emphases are important. First, owners and tenants must clearly and objectively understand the nature of soil erosion on their farmland. This includes the physical process and the economic costs and benefits of erosion control. Only with this information can the landlord start to formulate a site-specific benefit-cost comparison. Attempts to persuade landowners and tenants that conservation is a "good" thing without sound data may succeed in the short run. But the approach will ultimately fail when the parties discover the real benefits and costs. As explained, certain types of landlords, for example, nonoperators without farming experience, should benefit most from this information.

The second component is to provide both parties with model leases incorporating conservation cost-sharing provisions. Development of these model leases must be built from a thorough understanding of local and regional farmland rental markets. Lease recommendations that conflict with community custom or tradition will likely fall on deaf ears. For example, recommendations calling for a shift to crop-share leases from cash leases to promote conservation may not appeal to landlords in need of minimum cash flows, such as retired persons. One must understand that individuals generally are not in a position to change or dictate these customs or traditions. Instead, they respond to rental market forces. Recognizing these limitations, several provisions relating to conservation may deserve attention in the lease: (a) lease term, (b) specified conservation practices, (c) rules for sharing practice costs and benefits, (d) compensation for unexhausted improvements and damages, and (e) general do's and don't's of farming (19). The educational program should attempt to demonstrate how such a lease can work to the advantage of the owner and tenant.

3. *Research needs.* Leasing arrangements must allow landlords and tenants to share soil erosion control costs in proportion to the benefits they receive. Estimating the level and timing of conservation costs and benefits is not an easy task for knowledgeable owner-operators. When two parties are involved with rented land, each with different knowledge

bases, agreeing on acceptable cost-benefit sharing can be an enormous task. University experiment station and government agency research on the nature of practice costs and benefits is essential to promote landlord-tenant agreement. This will be a continuing task as agricultural economic conditions and technology change.

4. *Cost-sharing.* Despite efforts to carry out the program elements outlined above, land tenure constraints or related factors may thwart otherwise economically profitable erosion control practices. Rental market customs may preclude the sharing of erosion control costs and benefits. Landlords or tenants may face short-term cash-flow pressure. In those cases, cost-sharing subsidies can be targeted to help alleviate the constraint. This approach may be especially appropriate when constraints on landlords preclude their participation in soil erosion control and efforts must focus on tenants.

One practice possesses considerable potential in cases like this. That is conservation tillage. Separation of ownership from farm operation is not a constraint to the use of conservation tillage (*11, 17*). Presumably, this reflects the economic attractiveness of conservation tillage to operators from savings in time, fuel, and machinery costs. Where educational or technical assistance cannot overcome tenure constraints or other landlord-tenant characteristics, cost-sharing to encourage use of conservation tillage holds promise.

In Summary

Allegations that less erosion control is practiced on rented land than on comparable land operated by its owner have persisted for decades. If insecurity of tenure or problems with the incidence of conservation benefits and costs between landlords and tenants exist, this outcome is likely. Moreover landlords and tenants may possess certain characteristics that discourage erosion control investments (e.g., shorter planning horizon/ higher discount rate) in greater degrees than owner-operators.

Tests of the alleged erosion control problems have been fraught with conceptual and empirical problems. No uniform decision can be reached about the empirical importance of tenure and related considerations on soil conservation actions in all areas. Nonetheless, theory and some empirical evidence suggest that erosion control decisions on rented land differ from similar decisions by owner-operators.

Past soil conservation programs have been oriented primarily toward owner-operators. Because 40 percent of U.S. farmland is leased, a special program strategy for rented land seems sensible. Three major steps are involved:

1. Study and understand local and regional farmland rental market customs and traditions.

2. Identify what types of landlord-tenant situations exist and prioritize them on the basis of soil erosion control problems.

3. Develop rented land conservation program elements and apply them to specific landlord-tenant situations, depending on the existence of tenure or related constraints to erosion control.

REFERENCES

1. Barkley, Paul W. 1982. *Farmer attitudes and behavior associated with soil erosion control and structure of farming and land ownership in the future: Implications for soil conservation, a discussion.* In Harold G. Halcrow, Earl O. Heady, and Melvin L. Cotner [editors] *Soil Conservation Policies, Institutions, and Incentives.* Soil Conservation Society of America, Ankeny, Iowa.
2. Baron, Donald. 1983. *The status of farmland leasing in the United States.* In J. Peter DeBroal and Gene Wunderlich [editors] *Rents and Rental Practices in U.S. Agriculture.* The Farm Foundation, Chicago, Illinois, and Economic Research Service, U.S. Department of Agriculture, Washington, D.C.
3. Baron, Donald. 1981. *Land ownership characteristics and investment in soil conservation.* Staff Report AGES 810911. Economics Research Service, U.S. Department of Agriculture, Washington, D.C.
4. Berry, Russell L. 1964. *Share rents as an obstacle to farm improvement and soil conservation.* Land Economics XL: 346-349.
5. Bills, Nelson L. 1985. *Cropland rental and soil conservation in the United States.* Agricultural Economics Report No. 529. Economic Research Service, U.S. Department of Agriculture, Washington, D.C.
6. Bunce, Arthur C. 1942. *Economics of soil conservation.* Iowa State College Press, Ames.
7. Carlson, John E., and Don A. Dillman. 1983. *Influence of kinship arrangements on farmer innovativeness.* Rural Sociology 48(2): 183-200.
8. Dillman, Don A., and John E. Carlson. 1982. *Influence of absentee landlords on soil erosion practices.* Journal of Soil and Water Conservation 37: 37-41.
9. Ervin, Christine A., and David E. Ervin. 1982. *Factors affecting the use of soil conservation practices: Hypotheses, evidence, and policy implications.* Land Economics 58(3): 277-292.
10. Ervin, David E. 1983. *Incentives for practicing soil conservation: The influence of land tenure.* American Farmland Trust, Washington, D.C.
11. Ervin, David E. 1982. *Soil erosion control on owner-operated and rented cropland.* Journal of Soil and Water Conservation 37: 285-288.
12. Ervin, David E. 1981. *Soil erosion control on owned and rented cropland: Economic models and evidence.* Department of Agricultural Economics, University of Missouri, Columbia.
13. Gertel, Karl, Douglas G. Lewis, and Kenneth M. Miranda. 1985. *Investment in land by landowner classes.* Staff Report AGES 841 1029. Economic Research Service, U.S. Department of Agriculture, Washington, D.C.
14. Held, R. Burnell, and Marion Clawson. 1965. *Soil conservation in perspective.* Johns Hopkins Press, Baltimore, Maryland.
15. Hurlburt, Virgil L. 1964. *Use of farm resources as conditioned by tenure arrangements.* North Central Regional Publication 151. Nebraska Agricultural Experiment Station, Lincoln.
16. Lee, Linda K. 1980. *The impact of landownership factors on soil conservation.* American Journal of Agricultural Economics 62: 1,070-1,076.
17. Lee, Linda K., and William H. Stewart. 1983. *Landownership and the adoption of minimum tillage.* American Journal of Agricultural Economics 65(2): 256-264.
18. Norris, Patricia E. 1985. *Factors influencing the adoption of soil conservation practices in Virginia's piedmont bright leaf erosion control area.* M.S. thesis. Department of Agricultural Economics, Virginia Polytechnic and State University, Blacksburg.

19. North Central Land Tenure Research Committee. 1956. *Conservation on rented land in the Midwest.* North Central Regional Publication No. 69. Kansas Agricultural Experiment Station, Manhattan.
20. Schertz, Lyle P., and Gene Wunderlich. 1982. *Structure of farming and landownership in the future: Implications for soil conservation.* In Harold G. Halcrow, Earl O. Heady, and Melvin L. Cotner [editors] *Soil Conservation Policies, Institutions, and Incentives.* Soil Conservation Society of America, Ankeny, Iowa.
21. Wantrup, S. V. Ciriacy. 1968. *Resource conservation.* Division of Agricultural Sciences, University of California, Berkeley.

9

Barriers to Adoption of Soil Conservation Practices on Farms

Louis E. Swanson, Silvana M. Camboni,
and Ted L. Napier

American farmers receive international acclaim for achieving high levels of productivity and efficiency, but their successes have not been accomplished without environmental and social costs. Displaced farmers, eroded land, and polluted streams and lakes are some of the costs associated with the agricultural practices used to achieve such levels of productivity and efficiency.

Often, American farmers are aware of agriculture's adverse effects on the environment, and they usually recognize the social effects of people being forced out of farming. They also recognize the social pressures applied to the industry to produce high levels of output. Farm operators are constantly confronted with the dilemma of protecting soil resources or maximizing output to survive economically. Frequently, both objectives cannot be satisfied, which means that farmers must choose which goal to pursue. Most farmers, not surprisingly, opt to survive economically and act accordingly.

The American public must assume considerable responsibility for the soil conservation action by individual farmers because that public demands abundant, low-cost food and fiber products. The public also expects farmers to act as stewards of the land. Again, both expectations cannot be met simultaneously under existing socioeconomic conditions. Reilly captured the essence of the problem when he noted that U.S. farmers are encouraged to employ long-term planning horizons for soil erosion control and environmental protection but also are encouraged to use farming practices that degrade the environment to produce cheap food and fiber for domestic use and international trade (*33*). Reilly also noted that the public expects farmers to put the collective social good ahead of individual interests in terms of conserving soil. While some collective social interest can be expected of farmers, it is unrealistic to expect them to be concerned about soil erosion and off-site costs if the survival of their farm enterprises is threatened.

Soil Erosion as an Environmental Issue

More than 6 billion tons of soil are lost each year in the United States to soil erosion (*13*). Such a loss creates numerous socioeconomic and environmental problems for landowners and society generally.

A primary concern is the on-site cost of soil erosion. The cost not only varies but is unevenly distributed. Average soil loss per acre of cultivated land in the United States is about 8 tons per acre for all causes of erosion (*20*). The greatest portion of that soil loss is confined to a relatively small percentage of the land. About one-fourth of the nation's agricultural land is eroding at more than twice the established tolerance level (*35*).

Gardner argued that attention should focus more narrowly on about 10 percent of the land because that land contributes about 90 percent of the water-related erosion (*13*). While a large percentage of agricultural land appears not to be threatened by soil erosion, the portions of land noted by Sampson and Gardner are subject to degradation, if not destruction of their agricultural productivity potential.

The implication of these data for action is that targeting of programs to reduce soil loss on highly erodible areas is probably appropriate. Current expenditures for soil erosion control programs are unlikely to influence the problem significantly on a national scale unless these resources are directed to relatively few sites. In fact, it may be desirable to remove the 10 percent of highly erodible land from agricultural production. Perhaps the purchase of farming rights on this land or exclusion of such land from subsidy programs should be considered.

Micro targeting is probably justified because past claims that erosion adversely affects long-term soil fertility have been overstated. Crosson suggested that it was difficult to justify soil conservation programs on the basis of lost productivity nationally over the long term (*6*). He presented evidence indicating that the adverse effects of soil erosion on long-term fertility are relatively small. It is likely, however, that the high rates of soil loss on the 10 percent of highly erodible land are destroying its future productivity. Concentration of limited resources on these areas may prove to be cost-effective in reducing on-site and off-site costs.

On-site costs for individual farmers go beyond the loss of long-term fertility. A farmer may incur costs from such inconveniences as tilling land around eroded areas, forced retirement of highly erodible acreage, adverse effects on the aesthetic qualities of the farmstead, loss of chemical nutrients, and potential reduction in the land's resale value. Each of these costs might adversely affect the economic viability of the farm as well. Incorporation of the more immediate costs of soil erosion to the farmer into the development of information programs would probably result in more positive impact than arguments based on long-term fertility.

Off-site costs of soil erosion have received considerable attention of late. Deposition of soil in reservoirs, rivers, and road ditches affects many people beyond the boundaries of the land where the erosion occurred. Off-site costs of erosion are high because federal, state, and local governments must spend considerable sums of money to negate the effects of up-stream soil erosion. The Conservation Foundation estimates that off-site costs may be as high as $6 billion a year (6, 35). Among the off-site costs of soil erosion are the dredging of commercial waterways and highway ditches, purification of drinking water, loss of recreational use of streams and lakes, loss of fish and wildlife habitat, and a reduction in the aesthetic qualities of the environment (14, 30, 31).

Justification of action programs for soil erosion control will probably depend more on off-site costs in the future. Programs designed to inform landowners of the benefits and costs they incur from soil erosion control may have to rely more heavily on off-site costs. Landowners will have to be shown how they are harmed economically by the off-site costs of erosion for the program to have any impact. Demonstrating to up-stream landowners the adverse economic impacts on them from down-stream damages will be a difficult task.

While it is relatively simple to demonstrate that soil erosion is a serious socioenvironmental issue in the United States, it is extremely difficult to solve the problem. Efforts have been underway for decades to eliminate soil erosion, and even though some reduction in the extent of erosion has been noted over the years (13, 20), the problem persists. Leopold vividly described the negative effects of inappropriate land use that he observed in the early 1900s (21). He eloquently noted the potential environmental consequences associated with landowners ignoring their social responsibility to protect the land resource. Leopold's recommendations for action were largely ignored during his professional career and are primarily embraced by people today in an abstract manner. People generally believe the environment should be protected so long as there are no personal costs associated with the belief. Once personal costs are recognized, attitudes and behaviors become less supportive of environment protection. In essence, the problems identified by Leopold in the past still exist.

Farmers continue to use practices that degrade the land resource. They do so even when research shows they are aware of the erosion problem, believe they have a social responsibility to protect the land, possess favorable attitudes toward soil conservation, and often have the knowledge required to prevent soil erosion from occurring (*29, 31, 33, 36*).

These findings suggest that reliance on awareness programs to bring about adoption of soil erosion control practices is inadequate to solve soil erosion problems. Programs must be built on broader bases than simply creating favorable attitudes toward soil erosion control practices. Economic incentives have been used extensively to influence adoption because they affect the adoption behavior of landowners (*7, 8, 11, 12, 14, 27, 28*). Incentives, whether technical assistance or economic subsidy, reduce the risks associated with adoption. Such support also makes it possible for some farmers to implement soil erosion control programs that they cannot afford on their own.

While technical and financial support often encourages adoption initially, abandonment of practices can and does occur when subsidies are withdrawn. Unless incentives continue, farmers may reject the new conservation practices. This is especially true if conservation practices require considerable maintenance. Soil conservation practices may be discontinued also if they prove incompatible with other practices or technologies used on the farm. In addition, the purchase of new technologies may result in the destruction of conservation practices, such as terraces, if the newly acquired technologies are to be efficiently used.

Economic incentives are useful means of facilitating adoption, but provisons must be made to encourage the continued use of the practices once they are on the land. Action programs should not be terminated after adoption has occurred.

Evidence from awareness and information studies suggests that providing information to farmers, generating positive attitudes toward conservation, and developing beliefs that farmers are stewards of the land are necessary but not sufficient conditions to bring about the adoption of soil erosion control practices. In fact, awareness programs alone will prove ineffective generally in motivating farmers to adopt soil erosion control practices. Evidence indicates that farmers already are aware of the problem (*29*). Many farmers are concerned about soil erosion. They recognize the problem exists in their communities and even on their own farms. But most farmers, because of economic and market constraints, place high priority on productivity and efficiency criteria when making decisions about what farming practices to use. Short-term survival becomes the primary factor in governing decisions about the farming technologies and techniques used. Unfortunately, the most productive and efficient farming practices in the short run tend to have adverse effects on the land resource. Environmental concerns and a desire to protect soil resources are often relegated to a lesser priority. The outcome of this decision process is the use of farming practices that degrade land resources but maximize short-run profits.

Structural Barriers to Soil Conservation

Farmers generally opt to maximize short-run profits at the expense of land resource protection. Why? Because agriculture is a complex, highly competitive industry. The structure of the industry tends to dictate behavior among farmers. Farmers must increase their scale of operation and remain efficient. Survival demands it. Individuals who have access to land and capital continue to expand their farming operations. Those who cannot do so are soon forced out of farming. During the 1960s and even the inflationary 1970s, the scale of agriculture increased because of market pressures, technological growth, and relatively low real interest rates. High inflation made it possible to expand land holdings during the 1970s because real interest rates were low (35). This situation changed dramatically in the 1980s, when real interest rates rose sharply. Farmers who accumulated high debt ratios during the growth era suddenly encountered extreme difficulties. Oversupply of farm products resulted in low product prices, which reduced farm income. Agricultural land values began to decline, and the number of farmers with severe economic problems increased.

This brief history of the economic situation in agriculture explains in part why farmers do not adopt soil conservation practices. The economics of agriculture are not conducive to adopting soil erosion control practices because returns to investment in conservation are low and usually not realized for years (9, 18, 23). Farmers are motivated to survive economically. They are pressured by the competitive nature of the industry to adopt farming practices that maximize short-run profits. Rasmussen (32) and Margolis (24) articulated the situation well when they noted that farming decisions are often made to maximize short-run profits during periods of uncertainty. Farmers cannot be concerned about the future if they are not making enough money to cover their immediate costs. They will do whatever is necessary to survive in the short run. If they do not survive, of course, there is no long run.

When under economic stress, farmers will attempt to survive by ignoring soil erosion control practices or discontinuing practices that do not contribute to maximizing short-run output. Marginal land will be pressed into production; land devoted to such conservation practices as filter strips and crop rotation will be farmed; and existing land under cultivation will be farmed more intensely. Ironically, this solution of increased production, used most often to salvage farms in economic difficulty, is a major factor contributing to the problem.

Another structural factor that affects the conservation behavior of farmers is tax policy. Current tax policies subsidize conversion of marginal land to agricultural production (35). Additional acreage in production further aggrevates the problem of oversupply, which adds more pressure to people within the food system to expand productivity and become more efficient.

Farm support programs also contribute to the soil erosion problem. They encourage an increasing scale of farming when they are implemented without corresponding production controls (35). Under price support incentive systems, farmers strive to maximize production because a minimum price is established. When price support programs are combined with tax policies that encourage the purchase of production technologies, farmers tend to invest limited capital in technologies and land rather than in conservation practices. Ultimately, landowners become so immersed in the system that their production choices are practically predetermined. Farmers become instruments of the "technological treadmill" (5), and environmental considerations are de-emphasized even though individual farmers may be concerned about soil erosion problems.

Structural factors in the agricultural system are barriers to the adoption of soil conservation practices at the farm level. Evidence suggests that action programs designed to reduce soil erosion must consider modification of existing agricultural policies and programs. One action that must be taken on the policy level is the development of programs to reduce agricultural output (35). Elimination of incentives to keep marginal land in production will help remove some highly erosive land from production. Another action needed is revision of tax policies so that soil conservation farmers are rewarded and land resource abusers are penalized. More careful targeting of incentives to the most erodible areas appears appropriate, though such policies will not be politically popular with individuals who do not receive assistance.

Some form of cross-compliance to qualify for participation in subsidy programs should be examined also. Cross-compliance is one mechanism for elevating the priority of soil conservation among farmers. Caution must be exercised, however, in the use of cross-compliance. Some owners of highly erodible land may not have the resources to implement the actions necessary to qualify for program participation. If erodible land were eliminated by inactivity among landowners unable to qualify for participation, erosion control programs may not be applied to land most in need (10).

Individual Characteristics as Barriers to Adoption

Considerable research has been done in an attempt to understand how individual characteristics of farmers contribute to the adoption of soil conservation practices. The variables involved can be put into three broad categories: sources of information, personal characteristics of landowners, and farm structure variables.

Sources of Information. Traditional diffusionists assert that failure to adopt any object, practice, or technology is a partial function of being denied access to information (*22, 34*). That inability to access information, they argue, prevents individuals from being aware that potential solutions exist to perceived problems. Diffusionists believe that once farmers are aware of solutions that are advantageous for them to adopt, they will do so. Therefore, greater exposure to information sources will increase the probability that farmers will adopt soil conservation practices.

Personal Characteristics. Such individual characteristics of farmers as age, education, and experience relate significantly to adoption behavior (*26, 28*). Learning theory (*1*) suggests that younger people who have received their education within the recent past are more likely to adopt soil conservation practices because such farming techniques have been emphasized in their learning experiences. Older people learned about conventional tillage practices and other large-scale farming techniques that were the most appropriate practices during the time they received their formal education. Learning theory also suggests that older farmers tend to use practices that produced benefits in the past, especially short-run benefits. Practices that frequently maximize output are often the large-scale practices that negatively affect the environment. Evidence suggests, therefore, that younger farmers, with greater exposure to information sources and higher levels of education, are more likely to adopt conservation practices.

Farm Structure Factors. Individuals do not always behave in a way that is consistent with their attitudes. As a result, researchers interested in conservation adoption may have previously overlooked important barriers to adoption (*3, 15*). New evidence suggests that farmers may not adopt certain agricultural practices even though they have access to extensive information and have developed psychosocial attitudes that support adoption. The factor blocking adoption is the ability of farmers to act on their desires. In essence, farmers may not be able to adopt agricultural practices because of economic barriers (*3, 17, 28*).

Access to land and capital are often necessary to adopt different farming techniques (*2, 16, 17, 19, 28, 37*). For example, farmers who wish to shift from conventional farming practices to no-till or another form of conservation tillage may have to purchase new equipment, such as sprayers, chemical tanks, and planting implements. Farmers thus must have access to money if they wish to act on their desires to adopt different technologies and techniques (*3, 15, 28*). Farmers must also have farming operations that can accommodate the new practices (*34*). Large farms may be inappropriate for certain soil erosion control practices. For example, the practices may not be compatible with large farm equipment and certain tillage practices. This situation is discomforting because large farmers often have the economic resources to act if they elect to do so.

Risk is another factor usually ignored by social scientists interested in adoption behavior. The anticipated consequences of adoption decisions will affect whether or not an object, practice, or technology will be adopted (*4, 25, 26, 29, 31*). If farmers believe that adoption of soil erosion control practices will reduce the probability of survival, then they will not adopt.

Characteristics that Influence Adoption: An Ohio Sample

Data were collected from 918 farmers from nine Ohio counties in 1982. These data were to help determine what types of conservation practices the farmers were using. The data also were used to help build predictive models using personal and farm characteristics to explain the frequency of conservation practice use (*28*).

The study variables were selected from a variety of variables shown to be important to the adoption of soil conservation practices. The personal characteristics included agricultural education, age, use of alternative information sources, years engaged in farming, number of family members working on the farm, environmental attitudes, and number of organizations in which family members participate. The farm characteristics examined were type of farming operation (percent grain farmer, percent livestock farmer), measures of technology use (use of liquid application equipment on the farm, use of on-farm drying equipment, use of on-farm grain storage, horsepower of largest tractor, number of tractors owned, and number of combines owned), measures of farm size (acres usually farmed, number of acres owned but not farmed), and a measure of intergenerational transfer of farming knowledge and land (parents engaged in farming).

Ten tillage practices were evaluated in terms of their use frequency. The conservation practices included no-till, chisel plowing, crop rotation each year, crop residue left on the land, retirement of erodible land to grasses, stripcropping, grass waterways, and grass filter strips to stop sheet erosion. Conventional tillage practices included deep plowing and fall plowing. Farmers were requested to indicate how frequently they used each tillage practice. Multivariate analyses were used to build predictive models (*28*).

Several variables related significantly to use frequencies for several tillage practices. But the ability to predict use was relatively limited (explained variance was low). Both personal and farm characteristics were significant variables in all of the models. However, farm characteristics tended to be the best predictors.

Grain farmers were less likely to retire erodible land to grass and use other conservation practices, such as grass waterways, grass filter strips to stop sheet erosion, and no-till. Grain farmers also tended to use deep plowing more frequently.

Farmers with higher levels of agricultural education tended to use no-till more frequently, leave crop residues on the land, employ chisel plowing more often, retire erodible land to grasses, and adopt grass waterways more frequently.

The number of tractors owned entered two of the models. Farmers with more tractors tended to do slightly less fall plowing and use crop rotation each year more often. Tractor size entered four models. Farmers who owned larger tractors tended to chisel plow more frequently and do more fall plowing. They also were more reluctant to retire erodible land and use stripcropping.

Exposure to information systems and concern for environmental issues related significantly to several of the tillage practices. Exposure to information sources and environmental concerns tended to increase the use, though slightly, of conservation tillage practices.

Age, which entered one model, proved relatively unimportant as a predictive variable. Older farmers tended to use crop residue more frequently than younger farmers. Years of farming experience was also of little utility in explaining frequency of use of tillage practices. Experience entered two models (crop rotation each year and use of grass filter strips to stop sheet erosion). Farmers with more years of farming experience tended to use the two conservation practices slightly more often, which was counter to research expectations.

Surprisingly, size of farm was shown to be of little consequence in understanding the frequency of use of tillage practices. The number of acres farmed usually increased the probability, however slightly, that grass waterways would be used more frequently. The number of acres not farmed entered the no-till model and increased the probability slightly that no-till practices would be used.

The conclusion drawn from this research: Personal and farm characteristics do not adequately explain the frequency of use of conservation tillage practices. While farm characteristics tend to be the best predictors of the variables examined, the magnitude of the unexplained variance was high. But the study clearly indicated that reliance on information and educational programs to bring about adoption of conservation tillage practices is probably not very effective.

A second study was conducted using the same data. The focus of this investigation was the relative importance placed on four environmental concerns when farmers were making decisions about the adoption of farm technologies and techniques (*31*). Respondents were asked to rank the relative importance of water pollution, soil erosion, long-term fertility of the land, and impacts of adoption on wildlife in the decision-making process.

The results indicated that respondents tended to perceive environmental concerns as relatively important, but not as important as other factors, such as potential for economic return. Farmers who tended to be more concerned about the risk attached to adopting anything that could affect farm viability were also more concerned about the environment. This suggests that farmers who place more importance on environmental concerns when making adoption decisions about new technologies and techniques will probably be more cautious in the decision-making process. In other words, they may require more convincing. This explains why farmers may have positive attitudes toward the environment but still behave in a way that results in land and water degradation.

The only other variable to enter the model was the number of acres farmed. As cultivated acreage increased, concern about the environment decreased. In essence, farmers with a larger acreage tended to place less emphasis on environmental concern when making decisions about farm technologies and techniques than did farmers with a smaller acreage. This finding was expected. Large-scale operators probably have used intensive farming practices successfully in the past. They are also farmers who will likely continue to use techniques that produce results until those techniques cease to be productive. In other words, farmers will evaluate technologies and techniques in terms of productivity and efficiency rather than environmental concern.

Perceptions of Soil Conservation Issues in Kentucky

Research was conducted in Kentucky in 1982 to determine how farmers felt about soil conservation practices and what practices they had adopted (*36*). That study revealed that farmers tended to be favorable toward soil conservation programs, but few have conservation practices on their land.

The absence of conservation practices does not mean that farmers are unconcerned or do not recognize that a need for soil conservation exists. More than 90 percent of the 2,007 farmers included in the Kentucky study acknowledged that farmers were responsible for soil erosion control (*36*). They also believed that government involvement in soil conservation is acceptable so long as coercion is not used to force farmers to control soil erosion.

Several factors were associated with use of the eight conservation practices examined. Education and total family income related significantly to the use of all conservation practices evaluated. Farmers with more education and higher incomes tended to use conservation practices more often. Younger farmers used five of the eight practices more often. Farm characteristics associated with scale of farm operation did not correlate significantly with the use of conservation practices.

Interestingly, respondents reported that they believe conservation practices are profitable. In fact, a majority of respondents believed that every conservation practice examined was profitable. This finding questions the common explanation that farmers do not adopt conservation practices because they believe the practices are unprofitable.

The researchers concluded that factors other than those studied account for why farmers exhibit favorable attitudes toward conservation but do not adopt conservation practices. Economic constraints were among the items suggested for exploration. Farmers are unable to use limited economic resources for conservation practices, the researchers speculated, because those resources must be invested in technologies and techniques that will maximize short-run benefits.

In Summary

Individual characteristics and macro-level agricultural policies and programs influence the adoption behavior of farmers. Educational and information programs alone are inadequate to bring about adoption of soil conservation practices. Such efforts are necessary to make farmers aware of the threats posed by soil erosion and to demonstrate how they can address the problem. But these efforts are not sufficient to motivate farmers to invest limited economic resources in practices that yield few short-run benefits. Moreover, national farm policies contribute to the soil erosion problem by encouraging maximum farm production.

Resolution of the soil erosion problem apparently will require a combination of structural modifications and changes in behavior among farmers. Most emphasis in the past has been on bringing about changes in landowner behavior rather than addressing structural barriers. The relative ineffectiveness of past programs to resolve the soil erosion problem may be, in part, a function of the inattentiveness to structural constraints.

REFERENCES

1. Bandura, Albert. 1977. *Social learning theory.* Prentice-Hall, Inc., Englewood Cliffs, New Jersey.
2. Buttel, Frederick H., and Oscar W. Larson, III. 1979. *Farm size, structure and energy intensity: An ecological analysis of U.S. agriculture.* Rural Sociology 44(3): 471-488.
3. Camboni, Silvana. 1984. *The adoption and continued use of consumer farm technologies: A test of a diffusion-farm structure model.* Ph.D. dissertation. Department of Agricultural Economics and Rural Sociology, Ohio State University, Columbus.
4. Christensen, Lee A., and Patricia E. Norris. 1983. *Soil conservation and water quality*

improvement: What farmers think. Journal of Soil and Water Conservation 38(1): 15-20.

5. Cochrane, Willard W. 1979. *The development of American agriculture: A historical analysis.* University of Minnesota Press, Minneapolis.

6. Crosson, Pierre. 1984. *New perspectives on soil conservation policy.* Journal of Soil and Water Conservation 39(4): 222-225.

7. Ervin, Christine A. 1981. *Factors affecting the use of soil conservation practices: An analysis of farmers in Monroe County, Missouri.* M.S. thesis. Department of Geography, University of Missouri, Columbia.

8. Ervin, David E., and Charles T. Alexander. 1981. *Soil erosion and conservation in Monroe County, Missouri: Farmers' perceptions, attitudes and performances.* Department of Agricultural Economics, University of Missouri, Columbia.

9. Ervin, David E., and Robert A. Washburn. 1981. *Profitability of soil conservation practices in Missouri.* Journal of Soil and Water Conservation 36(2): 107-111.

10. Ervin, David E., William D. Heffernan, and Gary P. Green. 1984. *Cross-compliance of erosion control: Anticipating efficiency and distributive impacts.* American Journal of Agricultural Economics 66(3): 273-278.

11. Forster, D. Lynn, and George Stem. 1980. *Adoption of reduced tillage and other conservation practices in the Lake Erie Basin.* Technical report series. U.S. Army Corps of Engineers, Buffalo, New York.

12. Forster, D. Lynn, and G. S. Becker. 1979. *Costs and income effects of alternative erosion control strategies: The Honey Creek watershed.* North Central Journal of Agricultural Economics 1: 53-60.

13. Gardner, B. Delworth. 1985. *Government and conservation: A case of good intentions but misplaced incentives.* In *Soil Conservation: What Should be the Role of Government?* Indiana Cooperative Extension Service, Purdue University, West Lafayette. pp. 8-16.

14. Halcrow, H. G., E. O. Heady, and M. L. Cotner, editors. 1982. *Soil conservation policies, institutions and incentives.* Soil Conservation Society of America, Ankeny, Iowa.

15. Hassan, Salah. 1984. *Criteria for making decisions about adoption of new technologies: A test of a diffusion-economic constraint model.* Ph.D. dissertation. Department of Agricultural Economics and Rural Sociology, Ohio State University, Columbus.

16. Havens, A. Eugene. 1982. *The changing structure of U.S. agriculture.* In Don A. Dillman and Daryl J. Hobbs [editors] *Rural Society in the U.S.: Issues for the 1980s.* Westview Press, Boulder, Colorado. pp. 308-316.

17. Hooks, Gregory M., Ted L. Napier, and Michael V. Carter. 1983. *Correlates of adoption behaviors: The case of farm technologies.* Rural Sociology 48(2): 308-323.

18. Korsching, Peter F., and Peter J. Nowak. 1980. *Environment criteria and farm structure: Flexibility in conservation policy.* In Proceedings, Symposium on Farm Structure and Rural Policy. Iowa State University Press, Ames.

19. Lancelle, Mark, and Richard D. Rodefeld. 1980. *The influence of social origins on the ability to attain ownership of large farms.* Rural Sociology 45(3): 381-395.

20. Lee, Linda K. 1984. *Land use and soil loss: A 1982 update.* Journal of Soil and Water Conservation 39(4): 226-229.

21. Leopold, Aldo. 1966. *A sand county almanac.* Ballantine Books, New York, New York.

22. Lionberger, Herbert F. 1960. *Adoption of new ideas and practices.* Iowa State University Press, Ames.

23. Lovejoy, Stephen B., and F. Dale Parent. 1981. *The sociological study of soil erosion.* Department of Agricultural Economics, Purdue University, Lafayette, Indiana.

24. Margolis, Maxine. 1977. *Historical perspectives on frontier agriculture as an adaptive strategy.* American Ethnologist 4(1): 42-64.

25. Miller, William L. 1982. *The farm business perspective and soil conservation.* In H. G. Halcrow, E. O. Heady, and M. L. Cotner [editors] *Soil Conservation Policies, Institutions and Incentives.* Soil Conservation Society of America, Ankeny, Iowa. pp. 151-162.

26. Miranowski, John A. 1982. *Overlooked variables in BMP implementation: Risk, attitudes, perceptions and human capital characteristics.* In *Perceptions, Attitudes and Risk: Overlooked Variables in Formulating Public Policy on Soil Conservation and*

Water Quality. Staff Report number AGES820129. Economic Research Service, U.S Department of Agriculture, Athens, Georgia.

27. Moore, I. C., B.M.H. Sharp, S. J. Berkowitz, and R. R. Schneider. 1979. *Financial incentives to control agricultural nonpoint source pollution.* Journal of Soil and Water Conservation 34(2): 60-64.

28. Napier, Ted L., Cameron S. Thraen, Akia Gore, and W. Richard Goe. 1984. *Factors affecting the adoption of conventional and soil conservation tillage practices in Ohio.* Journal of Soil and Water Conservation 39(3): 205-209.

29. Napier, Ted L., and D. Lynn Forster. 1982. *Farmer attitudes and behavior associated with soil erosion control.* In H. G. Halcrow, E. O. Heady, and M. L. Cotner [editors] *Soil Conservation Policies, Institutions and Incentives.* Soil Conservation Society of America, Ankeny, Iowa. pp. 137-150.

30. Napier, Ted L., Donald F. Scott, K. William Easter, and Raymond Supalla, editors. 1983. *Water resources research: Problems and potentials for agriculture and rural communities.* Soil Conservation Society of America, Ankeny, Iowa.

31. Napier, Ted L., Silvana M. Camboni, and Cameron S. Thraen. 1985. *Factors associated with the importance placed on environmental concern in the adoption of farm technologies and techniques.*

32. Rasmussen, Wayne D. 1982. *History of soil conservation, institutions and incentives.* In H. G. Halcrow, E. O. Heady, and M. L. Cotner [editors] *Soil Conservation Policies, Institutions and Incentives.* Soil Conservation Society of America, Ankeny, Iowa. pp. 3-18.

33. Reilly, William K. 1984. *Soils, society and sustainability.* Journal of Soil and Water Conservation 39(5): 286-290.

34. Rogers, Everett M. 1983. *Diffusion of innovations.* The Free Press of Glencoe, New York, New York.

35. Sampson, R. Neil. 1985. *Government and conservation: Structuring an improved public role.* In *Soil Conservation: What Should be the Role of Government?* Indiana Cooperative Extension Service, Purdue University, West Lafayette. pp. 1-6.

36. Swanson, Louis E., and John F. Thigpen III. 1984. *Kentucky farmers' attitudes and behavior toward conservation.* Community Issues 6(2): 1-7.

37. Yapa, L. S. 1977. *The green revolution: A diffusion model.* Annals of the Association of American Geographers 67: 350-359.

10

Integration of Social and Physical Analysis: The Potential for Micro-Targeting

Stephen B. Lovejoy, John Gary Lee, and David B. Beasley

From the Dust Bowl of the 1930s to the present day, the American public has been reminded of the necessity for preserving soil and water resources. Programs have been advocated and policies initiated to influence farmers to use a variety of soil and water conservation practices. Reagan Administration officials in the U.S. Department of Agriculture have expressed concern about the future productivity of soil resources. The administration has initiated efforts to determine the best policy to conserve these precious resources.

Selection of an appropriate policy aimed at reducing soil loss on agricultural land requires that the policymaker know the environmental effectiveness as well as the social and economic impacts of alternative policies. But the constant monitoring of soil erosion is difficult and costly. Physical monitoring is usually impractical when estimating the environmental effectiveness of alternative control strategies except in research or demonstration projects. Even where good physical data exist, one deficiency of much conservation research is the absence of direct links between the environmental effects of alternative policies or programs and the socioeconomic impacts of the same alternatives.

A Local Perspective

Recent years have been exciting times in conservation work. A myriad of new initiatives have been advocated by observers, Congress, and the executive branch. Many of these proposed policies seek to use federal conservation funds more efficiently. But little analysis has been done on methods that local political divisions can use to increase the efficient use of the funds under their control, whatever the source of those funds.

The research reported here was developed, in part, to illustrate one method that local conservationists could use to increase conservation program effectiveness and efficiency. This analysis uses a hydrologic response simulation model to evaluate the effectiveness of several policy options for reducing soil loss in an actual watershed. Although control strategies, such as regulation or soil loss taxation, have been proposed to reduce the soil erosion, the emphasis of this analysis involves identifying potential differences in the effectiveness and efficiency of four voluntary soil loss reduction programs.

The Hydrologic Model

A model for simulating the impact of various erosion control measures would be useful in determining the cost effectiveness of alternative policies aimed at reducing soil loss from agricutural land. The model used in this analysis—ANSWERS (Areal Nonpoint Source Watershed Environment Response Simulation)—can generate site-specific information (1). It can also provide estimates of the overall effects of alternative control measures on soil loss throughout a watershed.

The underlying principle in the ANSWERS model is that at every point within a watershed fundamental relationships exist between the dependent processes of soil detachment, deposition, and loss and the governing hydrologic parameters, such as topography, storm intensity, soil types, vegetal canopy, and production practices (2). Use of this model requires that a watershed be divided into a grid system. The size of the grid's elements must be small enough so that all hydrologically significant parameters are approximately uniform within an element's boundaries. To account for spatial variation within the watershed, parameter values are allowed to vary between elements.

A Demonstration Watershed

To demonstrate the utility of this analysis, an agricultural watershed in central Indiana was selected. The Finley Creek watershed is located 10 miles north of Indianapolis. At the time of the study in 1982, a land survey of the 4,852-acre watershed indicated that about 90 percent of the land was in an agricultural use. Corn and soybean production accounted for more than 75 percent of total land use. This watershed is typical of central Indiana and many parts of the Corn Belt. Soils in the area tend to be silty clay loams or silt loams. Field slopes range up to 6 percent.

Interviews with all owners and operators in the watershed were conducted to determine current production practices as well as attitudes toward soil conservation policies. As part of the interview, respondents were asked to indicate the minimum subsidy payment necessary to alter their current production practices for specific five-acre elements under several policy scenarios. The elicited, site-specific subsidies were used to estimate the effectiveness and efficiency of each policy option applied to the Finley Creek watershed.

The analysis used the ANSWERS model to provide estimates of soil loss for each five-acre element in the watershed, given 1982 land use practices. These results were used to establish prioritized element rankings based on soil loss. The hydrologic simulation model was also used to estimate soil loss reductions from changes in production practices for various levels of participation under alternative policy programs.

Four Policy Options

A myriad of policies have been proposed to reduce soil loss from agricultural land (6, 7, 8). One proposal used recently is the targeting of federal resources (technical assistance and cost-sharing) to areas having high rates of soil loss. The various targeting proposals suggest a number of alternatives including new forms of cost-sharing to compensate farmers for shifting erodible cropland to less intensive uses. But there are questions about the effectiveness of these initiatives. A definite need exists to evaluate the impact of targeting policies at the local level, from both physical and socioeconomic perspectives.

The Finley Creek analysis combined the hydrologic simulation model and socioeconomic analysis to compare the efficiency and effectiveness of four voluntary subsidy programs aimed at reducing soil loss in an agricultural watershed. The four policies used in the analysis included a nontargeted subsidy for conservation tillage; a targeted subsidy for conservation tillage; a targeted, annual conversion subsidy (taking erodible land out of row crop production); and a targeted, permanent conversion program.

Under the nontargeted conservation tillage program, an annual subsidy was available on a first-come, first-serve basis to those individuals who adopted conservation tillage. No attempt was made to direct subsidies to those fields having large quantities of soil loss. To determine the effectiveness of a nontargeted subsidy program, a Monte Carlo simulation was employed to randomly select fields currently under conventional tillage practices. To simulate the environmental impact of adopting conservation practices within the watershed, hydrologic parameter coefficients, such as potential interception, percentage cover, surface roughness, and relative erodibility, were adjusted in the ANSWERS model to reflect soil and surface conditions representative of spring chisel systems now used in portions of the study area (*3, 4, 5*).

The second policy option, a targeted conservation tillage program, was similar to the nontargeted program. The difference involved the allocation of annual subsidies in a prioritized manner, based on soil loss predictions from the hydrological simulation model. Presumably, adoption of conservation tillage occurred on at least the field level (that is, fields containing one or more elements would alter tillage on the entire field). Annual subsidies were allocated on the same basis.

The third policy option was a targeted, annual conversion subsidy. The conversion program restricted corn and soybean production on very erodible, five-acre elements. A farmer was still allowed to produce non-erodible crops on these elements. The important factor in this option was that a farmer maintain a crop canopy on specific erodible areas. Unlike the conservation tillage program, the conversion subsidies were targeted to five-acre elements and not an entire field. The assumption here was that a farmer could continue present production practices on that part of

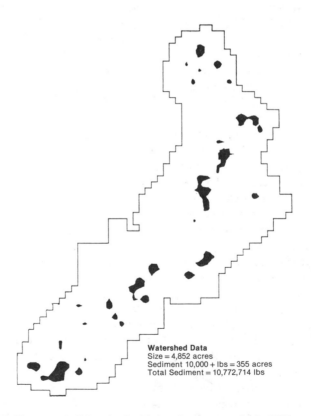

Watershed Data
Size = 4,852 acres
Sediment 10,000 + lbs = 355 acres
Total Sediment = 10,772,714 lbs

Figure 1. Soil loss in the Finley Creek watershed, 1982.

Table 1. Comparison of efficiency and effectiveness of four alternative soil conservation policies in Finley Creek.

Policy Alternative	Level of Participation (%)	Reduction in Soil Loss (%)	Estimated Direct Costs ($)
Nontargeted annual subsidy	1	.15	1,270
for conservation tillage	5	.98	6,109
	10	2.83	12,313
	15	4.41	18,470
	100	46.06	80,873
Targeted annual subsidy for	1	2.98	1,950
conservation tillage	5	11.96	6,875
	10	15.68	14,425
	15	21.68	20,875
	100	46.06	80,873
Annual subsidy for conversion	1	5.87	3,175
	5	13.95	17,800
	10	22.28	35,325
	15	25.66	49,800
	100	41.65	256,679
One-time payment for	1	5.87	59,750
permanent conversion	5	13.95	290,250
	10	22.28	574,150
	15	25.66	781,050
	100	41.65	4,133,608

the field not included in the targeted element.

The final policy analyzed was a targeted, permanent conversion program. Under this program, a one-time subsidy negotiated between the producer and the public body was used to purchase the right to produce erosive crops on five-acre elements having high soil loss rates. This proposal was similar to purchase of development rights or mineral rights.

How Effective the Policies?

Total soil loss in the Finley Creek watershed, given 1982 land use and production practices, was an estimated 5,386 tons. This represented an average annual soil loss rate of 1.1 tons per acre. Maximum annual soil loss per acre was nearly 28 tons.

Figure 1 illustrates the spatial distribution of soil loss greater than 5 tons per acre for 1982 land use and production practices. That year, 71 elements or 355 acres had a soil loss greater than 5 tons per acre per year.

To estimate the cost-effectiveness of each policy option, five levels of participation were considered. Participation was based on a percentage of the total land area, not the number of owner/operators. The cost estimate for each level of participation was derived by summing the acreage-specific subsidies (elicited by the respondents) necessary to induce each owner/operator to participate in each program.

Table 1 presents the estimated direct cost and predicted sediment yield reduction under each policy option in the watershed. All direct cost estimates were annual subsidies except the permanent conversion program.

At the lowest level of participation (1%) under the conservation tillage policy option, micro-targeting provided 21 times greater reduction in soil loss for only 50 percent higher direct costs (Figure 2). The differences between untargeted and targeted subsidies declined until the 15 percent level of participation was reached. Micro-targeting provided five times more reduction in soil loss at a cost that was less than 15 percent higher. To achieve a 25 percent reduction in soil loss over the 1982 baseline, the micro-targeting approach cost less than half as much as an untargeted program. In other words, for a $20,000 annual investment, the untargeted program would reduce soil loss 5 to 6 percent, while a micro-targeting program would reduce soil loss 21 to 22 percent in the Finley Creek watershed.

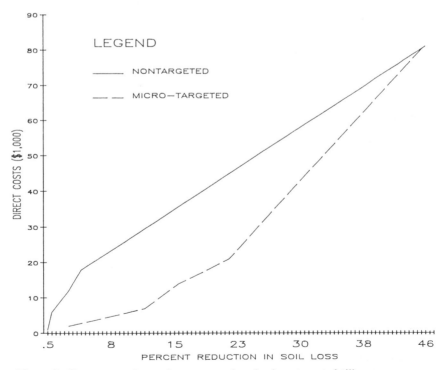

Figure 2. Cost comparison of nontargeted and micro-targeted tillage programs.

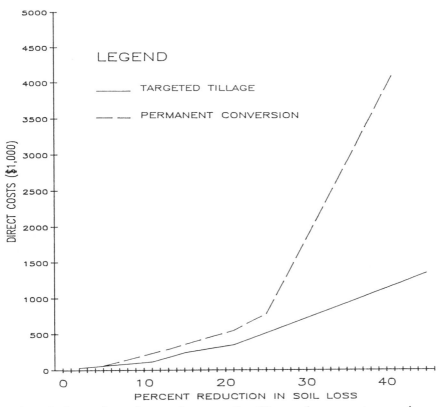

Figure 3. Comparison of targeted conservation tillage and permanent conversion policies.

Direct comparison of the efficiency of the permanent conversion program with the other alternative policies was difficult because of the different time horizons (annual payments versus a one-time lump sum). Therefore, a discounting technique was employed to make direct comparisons of annual subsidies and one-time payments. A variety of rates were used, from 2 percent to 10 percent. A 6 percent rate was ultimately chosen because separate analysis suggested that the weighted average discount rate of respondents was about 6 percent (4). In this analysis the site-specific annual subsidies were assumed constant and the number of subsidy years assumed infinite.

Figure 3 compares the effectiveness and efficiency of the targeted subsidy for conservation tillage and the targeted purchase of row-crop production rights at a 6 percent discount rate. These results suggest that, in general, the targeted conservation tillage program was more efficient means of reducing soil loss. Using a discount rate of 6 percent, the targeted conservation tillage program was significantly more cost-effective than the conversion program for soil loss reductions greater than 25 percent. For soil loss reductions less than 25 percent, the targeted conservation tillage program was only slightly less efficient than the permanent conversion program. But the comparison did not take administrative or enforcement costs into account.

If the discount rate is 6 percent and the desired soil loss reduction greater than 25 percent, the targeted conservation tillage subsidy program is definitely preferred. But if the discount rate is less than 6 percent or desired soil loss reduction is less than 25 percent, the permanent conversion program might be more efficient. The cost figures also indicated that the maximum reduction in soil loss from agronomic practices occurred under 100 percent participation in the conservation tillage program. At this level of participation, soil loss was reduced from the 1982 level by 46 percent.

The results of this applied analysis support the hypothesis that micro-targeting—the targeting of scarce financial resources to those specific areas within a watershed that lose large quantities of soil—would be a significantly more efficient and effective means of reducing soil loss from agricultural land within a given watershed. Moreover, under certain conditions, use of a permanent conversion program might be less expensive, especially if administrative costs were included.

A Useable Framework

Selection of policies and programs to control soil loss from agricultural land is complex and difficult. The analytical scheme suggested here is one way to conceptualize and measure the impacts of alternative policies. The integration of a hydrologic response simulation model with socioeconomic analysis provides a framework to assess the environmental effectiveness as well as direct costs of alternative policies. One promising policy option is the targeting of treatments to site-specific areas on the basis of a prioritized soil loss ranking (micro-targeting).

Although this analysis concentrated on agronomic practices (i.e., conservation tillage and conversion from row crops), the distributed parameter approach incorporated in the ANSWERS model is capable of determining the environmental consequences of implementing both agronomic and structural practices. This analytical framework of combined hydrologic and socioeconomic analysis can be used by federal, state, and local conservation agencies to estimate current levels of soil loss and determine effective management practices or incentives necessary to achieve a least-cost soil loss reduction strategy.

REFERENCES

1. Beasley, David B., and Larry F. Huggins. 1982. *ANSWERS user's manual*. EPA 905/9-82-001. U.S. Environmental Protection Agency, Chicago, Illinois. 54 pp.
2. Beasley, David B., L. F. Huggins, and E. J. Monke. 1982. *Modeling sediment yields from agricultural watersheds*. Journal of Soil and Water Conservation 37: 113-116.
3. Lee, John G. 1983. *Agricultural production and soil conservation: An analysis of the Finley Creek watershed*. M.S. thesis. Purdue University, West Lafayette, Indiana.
4. Lee, John G., Stephen B. Lovejoy, and David B. Beasley. 1984. *Soil loss reduction in Finley Creek: An economic analysis of alternative policies*. Journal of Soil and Water Conservation 40(1): 132-135.
5. Lovejoy, Stephen B., John G. Lee, and David B. Beasley. 1985. *Muddy water and American agriculture*. Water Resources Research 21(8): 1,065-1,068.
6. McConnell, Kenneth E. 1983. *An economic model of soil conservation*. American Journal of Agricultural Economics 65(1): 83-89.
7. Ogg, C. W., J. D. Johnson, and K. C. Clayton. 1982. *A policy option for targeting soil conservation expenditures*. Journal of Soil and Water Conservation 37: 68-72.
8. Williams, D. A. 1967. *Tillage as a conservation tool*. American Society of Agricultural Engineers, St. Joseph, Michigan. 56-57.

IV

Implications for Policy Development and Program Implementation

11

The Socioeconomic Dimensions of Soil and Water Conservation: Some Reaction

Richard Duesterhaus

My role is to comment on the implications for program implementation, though it will be difficult to avoid some overlap with research and policy development.

First, let me offer five general observations:

1. The symposium identified the state of the art and reinforced the idea or need for better integration of social and economic research with program and policy development and implementation.

2. Research has confirmed the validity of some current program approaches, while simultaneously singling out potential areas for improved program development and implementation.

3. The most helpful research seems to be that which helps set priorities on what should be done first in implementation to get the most return for the available resources.

4. Some overall umbrella, model, or conceptualization is needed that would help explain the various findings. The need is not for a rigorous mathematic model. There are obviously many data gaps. Perhaps a visual rather than a verbal presentation might be more effective.

5. The research indicates that there are some new approaches that can be taken to improve the efficiency and effectiveness of existing programs.

The complexity of the soil and water conservation issue is a challenge to the research community and to program implementors. First, multiple soil and water conservation problems exist. Soil erosion is only one aspect of the issue. Others include salinity, tilth, compaction, water managcment, and grassland management, just to mention a few. Solutions to these problems require a systems approach. Research on any one aspect may or may not be adequate to be generalized:

▶ We have multiple objectives or goals.

▶ We have multiple policies, programs, and activities.

▶ We have multiple tools and/or approaches (e.g., education, technical assistance, regulations, information, financial assistance, incentives, taxes, etc.). These are all needed in differing proportions in different situations. Some of these tools are not fully used or developed. Some of these tools are more appropriate for the different levels of our federal system. This especially needs to be recognized by researchers and policymakers as well as by program implementors. Regulation, particularly land use regulation, is more appropriately a state or local governmental tool, whereas tax policy can be useful at all levels. Some way of sharing between program implementors and researchers the many successes and failures in the uses of these various tools would be useful.

Obviously, more social and economic research is needed, followed by pilot studies and projects to replicate and test the results of the research. The findings of this work can be used to devise new national and state-wide approaches.

Some specific points or comments:

1. While the decision to have soil and water conservation and many other programs is a political and ethical one, the allocation of dollars available to program administrators must be guided by economic effectiveness measures.

2. Even though only 10 to 15 percent of the cropland may account for most of the erosion control problem on cropland, this represents a larger share of the farms and farmers than 10 to 15 percent. Erosion problems are not concentrated in one area. They are scattered throughout the country. The farmers and landowners in these areas are a diverse group with many different perspectives and attitudes about soil conservation.

3. Targeting is nothing more than a form of priority-setting. It is not a totally new phenomenon. It would be useful, though perhaps difficult, to set some priorities on social and economic research.

4. Institutions have been a key focus of this conference. Yet the use of "quasi" institutions—formal, informal, governmental, nongovernmental—needs to be addressed. Small hydrologic units as used here at the conference are but one example. Others would be steering committees, subdistricts of existing institutions, and other small groupings of farmers, ranchers, or other interested parties so as to facilitate communication and successful program implementation. It is similar to matrix management scenarios used for project management in government and private industry. New super agencies at the federal or state level do not really address or affect the need for small, workable institutions at the

program implementation or operational level.

One last comment has to do with the audience to whom we address our messages. A significant audience to address with the results of social and economic research includes program implementors themselves. While a small audience when compared to the millions of farmers and ranchers, the thousands of employees at the federal, state, and local levels are a major factor in the success or failure of conservation programs. To the extent they are better informed, we can expect better results.

Peter M. Tidd

Why does soil erosion continue? Sandra Batie discussed why from two perspectives, the "traditional" and an "alternative perspective." She focussed on property rights, macro-externalities, and agricultural production systems in an attempt to explain why it is difficult to implement soil and water conservation. Clearly, there is a need to expand traditional thinking and analyses for future conservation policy development.

Several speakers pointed out the need to look more at macro-economic and social factors that influence conservation policy. Institutional structure tends to be a barrier to soil erosion reduction. Soil and water conservation problems are long run, but subject to the impacts of short-run phenomena. The interrelationships of macro and micro variables must be understood to develop effective conservation policies.

The off-site impacts of soil erosion also deserve more attention in terms of quantifying specific interrelationships between on-site and off-site effects. This may require development of innovative conservation systems to reduce off-site impacts. It certainly will require an interdisciplinary approach to be most effective.

Some attention was given to moving from a voluntary approach to a regulatory approach as a means of solving soil and water conservation problems. By using current knowledge and by making some policy and program adjustments, significant progress can still be made through a largely voluntary approach. Knowledge gained about the concern and awareness of nonagricultural groups provides valuable information: these groups, along with agricultural groups, must be involved in the conservation goal- and policy-setting process at all levels of government.

There was some discussion about the lack of coordination between agencies, particularly within the U.S. Department of Agriculture, in solving soil and water conservation problems. This area needs to be better understood, but I think progress has been made in recent years. The soil and water conservation challenge is beyond one agency's scope. To get the job done agencies must work toward a common goal, not only at the federal level, but with state and local governments and interest groups.

Several points were brought out with respect to information needs and dissemination that deserve attention. The greater complexity of technology, along with farmers and landowners requesting more specific information about their individual situations, requires a new look at technology transfer. There is a need to increase information transfer to and through other organizations, interest groups, conservation districts, and commodity organizations. Advantage needs to be taken of conservation tillage clubs. Private information systems must be used. Total information packages, not bits and pieces, need to be developed that meet farmer and landowner needs.

Barriers and constraints to the adoption of soil and water conservation were touched on. Emphasis was placed on structural barriers. These barriers and their relationships must be understood. They vary by state and locality; they must be identified. From a policy perspective, land tenure and some other sociological relationships seem less important. These can be handled in program implementation.

Several points stand out that require attention by policymakers:

1. There is a need to look at the big picture—macro factors—particularly structural barriers. There must be a move away from traditional analyses.

2. More emphasis is needed on the off-site effects of soil erosion and the relationship of these effects to on-site erosion and soil and water conservation systems.

3. Coordination and cooperation must be improved within and outside U.S. Department of Agriculture. State and local involvement deserve emphasis in conservation policy development.

4. The compex technology of agricultural conservation alternatives must be recognized and information flow improved, particularly between research findings and implementation. The information needs to be timely and in a form that can be used.

5. Targeting as a policy is effective, but it may need some minor adjustments in implementation.

6. New strategies are needed for conservation implementation, beyond technical assistance, cost-sharing, and information dissemination. A closer look must be taken at the appropriate mix of technical assistance, cost-sharing, and information dissemination and their effectiveness in motivating conservation adoption under varying conditions.

Don Paarlberg

Soil and water conservation activities are in a state of transition. The change is from a past that is clear to a future that is uncertain, but full of promise. I see five areas of change: changes in practices, in attitudes, in objectives, in focus, and in delivery systems.

Changes in Practices. From 1976 to 1983, conservation expenditures for terraces, grass waterways, and gully control were reduced to one-fourth their earlier level. Meanwhile, the acreage in no-till cropping methods approximately doubled. This change is especially significant when one realizes that traditional practices were subsidized while no-till advanced, for the greater part, without government help.

What we are seeing is a fundamental change in tillage. For two and a half centuries we have been following the lead of Jethro Tull, the eccentric Englishman who taught the erroneous theory that soil had to be pulverized into tiny particles before it could be useful to plants. His enormously influential book, *Horse—Hoe—Husbandry,* helped to establish deep plowing and frequent cultivation, which contributed to soil erosion.

In recent decades we have found that crops can perform well without such tillage. Herbicides and insecticides have made it possible to control weeds and other pests with limited tillage. On sloping ground these new methods can reduce erosion as much as 80 percent. Furthermore, per bushel production costs with the new methods appear to be in the same range as per bushel costs with traditional tillage. While certain aspects of the new methods remain to be worked out, tillage methods clearly are undergoing transformation.

Changes in Attitudes. During most of its 50-year existence, the soil and water conservation movement was a crusade, intended to forestall the threat of ruined land and the inability to feed people. In 1938 Hugh Bennett, the father of soil conservation, remarked: "So direct, in fact, is the relationship between soil erosion and the productivity of the land and the prosperity of the people that the history of mankind, to a considerable degree at least may be interpreted in terms of the soil and what has happened to it as a result of human use."

By contrast, here is a statement made in 1985, in this book, by John Miranowski, director of the Natural Resources Economics Division of the Economic Research Service: "Over a hundred years time, soil erosion might cause an overall decline of 4 or 5 percent in productivity."

Changes in Objectives. When soil and water conservation programs began 50 years ago, the prime objective was to protect the productive capacity of farmland. Farmers were the major clientele group.

Now there is wide public concern about off-site effects, such as sediment deposition and the pollution of streams and lakes. While estimates are admittedly rough, it appears that off-site effects of poor resource use may be twice as great as on-site damage. Thus, a new and much broader interest has arisen in soil and water conservation. New agencies and new public actions have been launched in pursuit of these interests.

If a broad view of the objective is taken—protecting soil and water resources—then the new clientele provides greater support for the mission.

The new activities are allies of the Soil Conservation Service rather than rivals.

Changes in Focus. Public efforts to conserve soil and water were once applied widely in support of the feeling that such activities were appropriate on most farms. But studies have shown, as Swanson, Camboni, and Napier indicate in this book, that about 90 percent of the water erosion occurs on 10 percent of the land. Tighter budgets and concern about greater cost-effectiveness are demanding a sharper program focus. Targeting programs presents technical, administrative, and political difficulties, but such efforts appear to be in prospect.

Changes in Delivery Systems. The traditional institutions through which information on soil conservation is delivered have long been the local offices of the Soil Conservation Service, the soil conservation districts, and the Extension Service. But research has shown that new sources of information have increased in importance: farmer innovators, commercial firms, new agencies, and media with a nonagricultural orientation. How is the soil and water conservation movement to convey its message through these now less-structured channels?

Research and education will have to accommodate themselves to these changes. Figuratively, the payload, the vehicle, and the source of fuel are all in the process of change. Only the goal—protection of land and water resources—remains unchanged.

It is a new ball game. New tillage methods and the broader basis of concern about resource use give hope that the game can be won. But not with the old game plan.

C. Oran Little

This symposium provided an excellent forum for reviewing research, expressing concerns, and projecting ideas on the social and economic perspectives relating to soil and water conservation. As a representative of the state agricultural experiment stations, which have served a major role in developing the knowledge base to support a dynamic, successful agricultural industry in this nation over the past century, I was pleased to observe the thoroughness with which a team of superior scientists dealt with the subject. They identified continuing and significant problems, and they accepted the challenge of being a part of the solutions.

In essence, the problems concern management of the base resources, soil and water, which are critical to food and fiber production. The various pressures that influence conservation decisions in both the private and public arenas were presented. These pressures, embedded in economics, structure, education, and social values, are complex. Much remains to be done to determine just how they function individually and together, but a big step was made in laying them before us. We now have the opportunity to develop further the pertinent knowledge bases, to expand the circles of the informed, and to implement solutions. History clearly dictates that management of these resources will shape the future of society.

I do not see clearly a pathway for immediately improving soil and water conservation. But I am confident that the research community has the capabilities to provide the necessary knowledge base; the necessary service agencies exist to disseminate information effectively; and the clientele is eager to apply the required management with proper incentives. Priorities must be established, investments made, goals set.

This symposium focused strongly on policy development and program implementation. There was an excellent overview of contrasting philosophies concerning property management and land rights. Who pays and who receives? Where do investments originate? Where are benefits to be realized? Such questions are fundamental to policy development. Are we prepared to focus needed research on relative costs and benefits, options and alternatives, consequences of change or no change? Will a solution to one problem create more problems in associated areas?

The jury is still out on the economics of soil and water conservation. One might believe that we cannot afford to make the investments, but the consequences of not doing so are unacceptable. Are we really basing tomorrow's economics on yesterday's technologies? There are exciting new technologies on the horizon that could affect conservation economics. Clearly, too, not all values can be quantified in dollars and cents.

The structure of American agriculture continues to be a serious policy issue. If I interpret correctly the information relating conservation to structure, effective conservation is favored by the "family-farm." This certainly needs further study. It may well become a major consideration.

Much has been said about what is not being done in soil and water conservation. Perhaps we are too quick to emphasize how empty the cup and too slow to acknowledge how full the cup. Obviously, considerable work has been done, and success has been experienced in conservation. Clearly, a majority of farmers are indeed using effective conservation practices on most of this nation's cropland. Targeting of programs has come of age, and recent pilot efforts appear to have been successful.

Finally, this symposium further intensified the realization that advancements in soil and water conservation will depend on people. People who are dedicated to sustaining food and fiber production capabilities, people involved in various areas of society who recognize their unique responsibilities in partnership with others, people anxious to build on accomplishments by being proactive rather than reactive, and people who focus on the possible will eventually develop the policies and implement the programs. The oganizers of this symposium and its participants are that kind of people.

12

The Socioeconomic Dimensions of Soil and Water Conservation: Some Discussion

Micro and Macro Factors Influencing the Adoption of Soil and Water Conservation Practices

Cameron S. Thraen, Ted L. Napier, and James A. Maetzold

Micro and macro factors may influence the formation of soil conservation policy and the design and implementation of soil conservation programs and practices. These factors can be grouped under two main headings. First are those relating to policy and program design. Second are those ideas concerned with program implementation.

Policy and Program Design

What is the efficacy of conservation policy and program design based on the traditional notion of micro or private valuation of conservation practices? This traditional notion holds that the costs of soil erosion accrue mainly to the landowner or land user; as such, any decision on conservation is properly a private and voluntary one. This view is rooted in a long history of private property rights and the idea that on-farm costs of soil erosion are borne directly by the landowner and only incidentally by society at large.

Of concern are the numerous macro or aggregate factors that impact on an individual's conservation decisions. These macro factors include basic economic conditions in the farming sector, foreign exchange rates, tax provisions, and so forth. The factors may play an important role in determining the success or failure of specific policies or programs based only on consideration of micro factors. Current policies or programs do not include provisions to incorporate or react to macro-variable influences. There needs to be greater awareness of this in making soil conservation policy and designing conservation programs. Current social and economic research has dealt in large part with improving knowledge of conservation decision-making at the micro level. Research must be extended to include linkages between soil conservation decisions and the influence of macro variables.

Focusing mainly on the on-site costs of soil erosion helps keep current policy and accompanying programs directed toward the individual as the decision unit. But current research suggests that such micro concerns as soil productivity loss will not be a significant influence on the individual decision to practice soil conservation. The more important question may be the extent of off-site erosion costs. A shift of research focus to the question of off-site costs may help soil conservation policy shift toward more macro-oriented programs.

Another concern is that policy goals often conflict. At the micro level, the question of soil productivity loss is squarely set against the issue of long-term economic viability of the farming unit. Soil productivity loss in most areas is a gradual factor for which private discounting generally leads to the conclusion that additional investment in soil conservation technology has little or no return. Another issue is the potential conflict between the policy goal of conservation tillage and soil compaction, along with increased use of pesticides. Conservation tillage reduces soil erosion while possibly increasing the potential for groundwater pollution.

There is also the potential for conflict between those goals aimed at the micro aspects of soil erosion control and agricultural goals in general at the macro level. The policy of an abundant, cheap food supply ensures that rates of return to agriculture will be low over time. But this policy also ensures that the economic incentive to adopt soil-conserving practices will also be low. Alternatively, high market prices and rates of return lead to intensive cropping and land use.

A final concern is the relationship between conservation policy and global food needs. How does one justify programs that reduce productive output, programs such as the proposed conservation reserve, while the need for food is expanding worldwide?

Development of soil conservation policy and design of programs can benefit from more information relating micro-level benefits and costs to macro-level variables that influence conservation decisions and yet are not themselves directly affected by soil conservation policy. Program design needs to deal with soil erosion problems at the margin, not the average. This calls for the design of programs that are more targeted and that consider the potential goal conflict that may occur.

Finally, development of policy and design of programs may need to be approached more from the perspective of a public good and less from the traditional view of private ownership. This shift in the policy perspective—to view national food and fiber productivity as a common property resource—will create new areas for debate about the proper regulatory role of government.

Program Implementation

On the issue of program implementation, a number of ideas provide the focal point for discussion. Current institutions in the soil conservation arena need to be imbued with a broader perspective. This perspective must account for macro variables and their influences as well as micro variables. Also, there must be greater awareness of the fact that cooperation among agencies and institutions is essential to the success of any conservation program. This cooperation applies not only to the traditional actors in soil conservation but also to nontraditional actors at the macro level. Policy designed to enhance commodity prices and expand product markets must consider soil conservation implications.

Soil conservation agencies need to be setting policy, designing programs, and implementing these with the cooperation of the many other agencies and institutions that affect the well-being of the agricultural sector. Successful program implementation requires that these programs work at the watershed level. The potential for success is greater when programs are targeted to the soil conservation problem as it exists at the margin and not as an average concept. Using an average perspective only serves to dilute the program effort.

A significant difficulty with achieving success under current programs is the fact that private rates of discount do not coincide with social rates. The benefits that accrue as a result of soil-conserving practices from the individual's point of reference are far less than those from a social perspective. If these two views are to be more closely aligned, which would contribute more to conservation objectives, there must be stronger emphasis on public education. The conservation ethic needs to be renewed and strengthened. This may also require greater educational efforts in the nation's school systems and land grant institutions.

Conclusion

Current conservation policy needs to consider the significant influence of macro variables. Success in soil conservation programs may rely more on variables over which the programs have little or no control.

Off-site costs of soil erosion may substantially outweigh the more traditional on-site costs. This may, in turn, require that policy take on a more direct involvement in the conservation decision. The public good may dictate a regulatory environment as opposed to the current participatory environment. This may become even more compelling as conflicting conservation goals become more apparent.

Finally, there needs to be renewed interest in strengthening the conservation ethic. This calls for an increased policy and program efforts in public education and awareness of soil conservation issues.

Information Needs and Dissemination

Steven E. Kraft, William Alex McIntosh, and Edgar Michalson

What information do farmers need to practice soil conservation? How should agencies disseminate such information? These questions have implications for policy development, program implementation, and future research.

Information Needs

Information must be of a variety to fit the needs of a heterogeneous social and physical environment. Farmers differ greatly from one another. For instance, they can be distinguished as innovators, early adoptors, early majority, late adoptors, and laggards. Each of these groups have differing needs in terms of information type, amount, and timing. For example, information regarding more risky forms of technology must be directed toward innovators. Other types of farmers may prefer information regarding less risky innovations.

Agencies must focus on what is called the critical 10 percent of the agricultural population. These farmers are not innovators or early adoptors; they are part of the large group labeled as the early-late majority. These are farmers who need a little prodding to induce them to accept conservation practices that have already been successfully demonstrated by the innovators and early adoptors. This 10 percent is important in "pulling" late adoptors along.

Information also needs to be targeted to deal more effectively with differences found across the United States and within local areas. Innovations that work well in Idaho and Washington may fail in Iowa. In addition, farmers need site-specific information, not only to persuade them of their soil erosion problems but also to provide them with viable recommendations for dealing with these problems.

The naive assumption that awareness of soil erosion will lead to adoption of soil conservation practices must be abandoned. This type of approach must be replaced by information about on-site productivity effects and managerial impacts, along with data about off-site costs and benefits. Consequently, governmental agencies must be able to demonstrate the negative internal and external effects associated with soil erosion. Furthermore, agencies must be able to verify linkages between on-farm activities and off-farm effects. These must include the links between farm-based soil erosion and off-farm costs as well as the links between conservation activity on the farm and off-farm benefits.

There is also a need to target information that demonstrates the extent to which soil erosion and soil conservation affect land values. Such effects will be influenced by cropland location vis-a-vis urban areas, soil characteristics, and the farm enterprise mixes in an area.

Disseminating Information

Targeting may also require new methods of disseminating information. One approach used by business firms may have some applicability. Market segmentation divides heterogeneous customers into homogeneous groupings. Knowledge about the characteristics of these groupings, such as risk-bearing ability, economic situation, and level of information need, permits firms to tailor information packages accordingly.

Problems of information dissemination are part of a wider communication concern. Agencies must reassess the methods they use to communicate among themselves and with farmers. This reassessment also entails a critical examination of the division of labor among agencies. Additional research is needed, however, to pinpoint administrative alterations. Interorganizational research and network analysis are two approaches that may provide some answers.

Several perceived problems prompted these recommendations. First, agencies, particularly the Cooperative Extension Service, tend to lag behind farmers' needs. For instance, in some areas no-till has been promoted largely by farmers. Occasionally, this has occurred against the advice of university personnel, who feel no-till is uneconomic.

A second problem involves networks of farmers themselves, particularly among innovators. Innovators apparently rely on one another for moral support, encouragement, and information. Pinpointing such networks and locating "opinion leaders" among the members would facilitate unmet information needs and possibly make innovators even more innovative.

Finally, there needs to be an expansion of agency support personnel. People with interest and expertise in off-site damages and water quality issues need to be brought into agencies. In some people's view, the Soil Conservation Service has moved away from its holistic, ecological approach to resource planning and many conservation districts have pulled away from their mandated role in resource planning within their jurisdictions. Inclusion of more environmentally based groups would be a "soft" approach to confronting agriculturalists with the reality of gradually changing property rights. Contact between farmers and environmentalists would also foster dialogue between the groups, hopefully resulting in the agency perspective shifting from one of defending agriculture to a pro-active stance encouraging adjustments in production agriculture to reduce off-site impacts. The contact might also sensitize farmers to the problems of off-site damages, the political and financial pressures such damages engender, and the possibility of these pressures leading to a restructuring of property rights. Ideally, with the contact, gradual adjustment and accommodation would take place.

Conservation agencies could take a leading role in this effort. In some areas of the country, where conservation district and SCS personnel have taken active roles in helping counties deal with the technical aspects of the permitting process for mine reclamation, some models for this kind of agency staff-environmentalist interaction might already exist.

Also, while the work of conservation agencies is technical in nature, personnel must be willing and able to assume the mantel of a sales person or promoter. This means developing the skills to make personal contacts, determining where to make contacts using approaches that will not put off the potential client, and learning what works with farmers and/or landowners. Indeed, acceptable strategies might well differ by specific client groups. Similarly, agency personnel must follow up contacts made with farmers and previous recipients of technical assistance. Just as equipment dealers develop accounts that are monitored, so must conservation personnel. A problem may arise with this suggestion because some agency personnel do not believe they should be engaged in sales. In this case, agencies must develop a division of labor, enlisting their more gregarious members to meet farmers and landowners initially.

Not only do farmers and agencies continue to have their information needs unrequited, so do social scientists. A good deal more must be learned about what motivates conservation behavior among farm owners and operators. While research shows that information is important in describing conservation behavior, that information per se is a poor predictor of conservation activity. This reality leads to two recommendations. The first involves the need for more complex, theoretical models to use in predicting conservation activity. The second is the need to better define a broad-based conceptual model that portrays the multitude of factors contributing to soil conservation behavior. The model is seen as important for organizing existing data, indicating areas of inadequate information, illustrating how relations and interactions might change by geographical location and/or farm type, and demonstrating the need for information on off-site effects. Such a conceptual model could be important in identifying institutional barriers, socioeconomic constraints, and political limitations to the conservation process.

Information is sorely lacking on off-site effects of soil erosion. Coupled with the paucity of data about the positive and negative impacts of on-farm soil erosion and its control, additional research is needed on model development and data collection. At least from the farm-level perspective, there is a need to evaluate soil erosion and its control in the whole-farm context and not just from the perspective of making a soil map of a field.

Constraints to Conservation

Thomas J. Hoban IV, Eric Hoiberg, and Barbara Osgood

Many experts believe that soil erosion problems are worse today in many parts of the country than at any time in history. After 50 years of educational programs, financial incentives, and technical assistance, it is reasonable to ask why we have not solved erosion problems. We need to ask what we can try now that will motivate more farmers to voluntarily adopt soil and water conservation practices. To effectively promote soil and water conservation, we must understand the constraints to conservation program effectiveness as well as farmers' abilities to practice conservation.

Constraints to Conservation

Most farmers are concerned about soil erosion and pesticide loss. They generally are willing to help solve soil erosion problems if given options without penalties. Various constraints, however, limit many farmers' abilities to practice adequate soil conservation.

The current economic condition of American agriculture poses definite constraints to soil conservation. Planning horizons are short. With increased emphasis on cash flow, many farmers are unable to commit scarce resources to conservation, and banks may be unwilling to lend farmers the additional money needed. Falling land prices may also work against conservation. When land is worth less, farmers' incentives to practice conservation may also be less.

Relationships between landlords and tenants are often cited as a major constraint to conservation. Many local conservation professionals and conservation district board members state that absentee ownership is the main cause of soil erosion problems. But some research shows little evidence of such a simple relationship.

Another potential constraint is part-time farming, which is becoming more common in many parts of the country. Part-time farmers derive income from nonfarm sources, so they may consider farming as only another business enterprise. Also, small-scale, noncommercialized farmers may be unwilling or unable to participate in conservation assistance programs.

Strategies for Promoting Conservation

Ongoing conservation education efforts remain a vital and viable strategy for promoting conservation. But the perceived need for education must precede education.

Educational and assistance programs must be tailored to different groups of farm owners and operators. Promotional strategies should be different for an owner-operator than for a landlord and tenant. To promote conservation tillage we need to target the farm operator. For land diversion or structural practices, on the other hand, we need to reach the landowner. Leases requiring conservation tillage may have potential for conservation-minded landowners who do not operate their farms.

In addition to production concerns, some farmers consider conservation a consumption good. They like to see terraces and stripcropping. Also, most farmers want to feel a part of their community. They want their community to be a nice place to live. They consider conservation as something they do for their community. Certain rewards and recognition would help ensure long-term maintenance of conservation systems.

Local involvement and investment in conservation programs will become increasingly important as the federal role shrinks. Local leaders are in the best position to determine needs and get people involved in conservation programs. Also, nonfarm audiences need to be targeted and provided with conservation information. For example, politicians and their staffs at all levels of government need conservation information.

All citizens, especially the 97 percent who do not live on a farm, need to recognize our dependence on soil and water. In the United States, where land is abundant, we have felt that enough land is available to replace what has been destroyed by soil erosion. As a result, much of our topsoil is gone in many locations.

Policy Implications

Drastic action is needed in certain highly erodible areas. Where severe soil erosion problems are identified, the land should be removed from row crop production. We can't miss the present opportunity to enact land retirement (i.e., conservation reserve) legislation. Many farm and environmental organizations are supportive now, but might not be under other conditions. They also feel that the potential exists for merely switching bad management from one area to another unless a sodbuster provision is tied to any conservation reserve policy.

Increased emphasis is needed on regionalization and less generalization to the nation as a whole. The relative roles of federal, state, and local governments in conservation must be redefined. If the federal role becomes smaller, state government will need to assume a greater role in terms of funding, educational support, and overall leadership. Local government (i.e., districts) must also be revitalized. Teamwork at the local level, involving both the private and public sectors, will be important for effective district programs.

In addition to farm operators, conservation professionals and district leaders should also be seen as adopters of new programs and ideas. We need to understand how the adoption process relates to their decisions. They need encouragement to adopt innovative strategies to promote conservation. New strategies for some local areas might include targeting specific audiences with integrated educational campaigns; setting up informal farmer networks, such as no-till clubs; and having various organizations work together actively as a team. New ideas also need to diffuse, such as the complexity of the landlord tenant situation or the use of micro-targeting.

Extension's role in farm management education should shift more toward conservation and away from production. Extension has the information delivery system and community linkages in place to promote conservation more effectively. Local extension workers need to work more closely with conservation districts and local conservation professionals to provide information on the costs of soil erosion and the benefits of conservation.

Use of watershed modeling may allow local staff to identify "hotspots" based on the type of practices, terrain, and hydrology. While watersheds are the most important and natural unit for planning and programming, the political world makes it difficult to overcome county boundaries. The potential for conflict between county systems and any proposed hydrologic unit system is certainly a factor to consider.

An important omission in the past has been the determination of which agency will serve as the diffusion agent for new policies and programs. Also needed are strategies for improving the adoption of strategies to promote conservation by local leaders and conservation professionals. We need to identify and overcome the barriers that limit local adoption of innovative programs and policies.

Information and Research Needs

The important influences of macro-level economic factors on conservation have been recognized. But we lack a clear understanding of the specific impacts of structural factors on conservation program effectiveness and farmers' adoption of conservation practices. Interrelationships among conservation, economic, and social policies and programs are complex. The effectiveness and equity of alternative conservation policies, at all levels of government, need to be examined. Policies not directly related to conservation should also be assessed for their potential impacts on conservation.

In reality, local leaders and conservation professionals have little influence over these macro-level factors. But it is important to understand and make recommendations about the factors that they do have control over, such as program delivery, interorganizational coordination, local district leadership, community involvement, and promotional strategies. Research and application are needed in each of these areas.

Innovative programs and policies are developed across the country at both state and local levels. Some central clearinghouse and diffusion network should be established to collect, synthesize, and report on successful state and local conservation initiatives. This system could be similar in many ways to the Conservation Tillage Information Center.

Specific program and policy questions that future research must address seem numerous. Following are but a few suggestions:

► How can districts become more visible and effective?

► What are the most effective educational and assistance strategies for different groups of farm operators?

► What changes need to be made in our institutions?

► Should we work within hydrologic units (i.e., watersheds) rather than districts (i.e., counties)?

► How do the trends toward off-farm employment and part-time farming influence adoption of soil and water conservation practices?

► How do community social, economic, and political systems influence conservation decisions?

► What kind of generalizations can we draw from social science research that will be most useful for policy development and program implementation?

► What are the political ramifications of targeting?

► How does the current Agricultural Stabilization and Conservation county committee structure determine program implementation?

► How do we know what types of resources (e.g., funding, staff, and information) we need?

► If we accept a zero-sum game, how can we increase resources for conservation?

► How does the land market reflect use of conservation practices?

► How are reasonable and acceptable levels of shadow pricing established?

► What benefits other than income are derived from the establishment of wildlife areas for hunting?

► What impacts do the major nonfarm sources of sediment have on stream water quality?

▶ How does upstream land treatment affect streambank erosion through changing runoff patterns?

Conclusions

An interdisciplinary approach is needed for conservation policy research. Emphasis on interdisciplinary research implies use of a systems model. This will be especially beneficial for understanding and documenting off-site benefits and costs. Such an approach is compatible with and could be modeled after the emerging farming systems perspective. A systems approach would also be consistent with SCS emphasis on resource management systems.

We need to examine critically how much variation in conservation adoption is really explained by any one of the typically used variables. It seems questionable how much return on scarce research funding we will receive from a continued focus on only the personal and farm firm characteristics that influence farmers' conservation decisions.

Society cannot wait for the farm economy to change for the better before conservation receives greater recognition. Conservation tillage and the conservation reserve are both economically rational and technically effective options. The challenge is to apply scientific models of organizations, interorganizational relations, communities, communication, and innovation diffusion in promoting conservation.

Index

Adoption, of conservation, 114, 136, 140-150
Agricultural policy, U.S., 3-12
  analysis of, 121-128
  conservation and, 22-24
  environmental consequences of, 109, 112, 123, 128
  farm bills and, 26, 49
  information needs, 55-69
  interagency cooperation, 45-46
  international trade and, 62-63
  local involvement in, 47-51, 63-64, 147-148
  macro variables, 15-24, 141
  multidisciplinary aspects of, 64
  public policy context of, 26-37
  regulation and, 28-29, 134, 147-148
  research and, 121, 148-150
  state-local coordination and, 63-64
  structural factors of, 148
  tax policy and, 18, 22-23, 34, 66, 113, 134
Agricultural Research Service, 40
Agricultural Stabilization and Conservation Service, 85
  county committee structure, 149
  as information source, 76-78
  SCS and, 42-43, 45
Agriculture:
  cyclical nature of, 35
  economics of, 5-8, 32, 36, 56-60, 96, 112 134, 150
  resource degradation and, 26, 28-29. (See also Pollution)
  structure of, 139
  (See also Farms)
Air pollution, off-farm, 3
American Agricultural Economics Association, 66

American Society of Agricultural Engineers, 57
American Society of Agronomy, 57
ANSWERS. (See Areal Nonpoint Source Watershed Environment Response Simulation)
Areal Nonpoint Source Watershed Environment Response Simulation, 122-123

Bennett, Hugh, 137

Chemicals:
  productivity and 34-35
  runoff, 28
Chisel plowing, 115-117
Commodity programs, 35
Compensation, property rights and, 11
Compliance:
  cross-compliance programs, 12, 66, 113, 135
  voluntary programs, 9-10, 28-29, 37, 71, 81
Conservation districts, 47-51
  associations of, 48
  marginal criteria and, 57
Conservation Foundation, The, 61, 110
Conservation programs:
  adoption practices, 114 136, 139-150
  constraints to, 56-62, 146-150
  design of, 140-142
  impacts of, 121-128
  information sources for, 74-82
  land tenure and, 95-106
  local involvement in, 45-51, 147-148

macro economics of, 15-24
policy analysis, 4-12, 26-37, 123-128
regional effects of, 60
research directions for, 148-150
simulation model of, 122-128
socioeconomics of, 133-150
state involvement in, 47-51, 63-64
structural barriers to, 112, 114-115, 136, 149
U.S. Department of Agriculture plans, 73
voluntary compliance with, 9-10, 28-29, 37, 71, 81, 135
Conservation Reporting and Evaluation System (CRES), 43
Conservation tillage. (*See* Tillage programs)
Conservation Tillage Information Center, 23, 149
Contour seeding, 65, 84
Cooperative Extension Service, 43-46, 138, 143
  conservation focus of, 148
  information programs of, 76-78
Cost-benefit analyses, 56-60, 139, 150
  of conservation, 5-8, 96, 134
  of erosion, 29-30, 56-62, 109-110
  simulation model for, 122-128
  of water pollution, 11
Cost-sharing programs, 4, 6, 9, 11-12, 27, 29
  as incentive, 136
  landlord-tenant, 105
  state, 51
  targeting of, 40-51, 123-125
County agricultural centers, 45
CRES. (*See* Conservation Reporting and Evaluation System)
Crop rotation, 65, 115
Crop yields:
  erosion rates and, 5
  tillage programs and, 65, 67-68
Cross-compliance programs, 12, 66, 113, 135

Disaster programs, 11

Economic Research Service, 20, 40, 137
Education programs, 7, 24, 104
  changes in, 138

promotion of, 146
(*See also* Information programs)
Environment:
  erosion and, 109-112
  impact of conservation on, 123
  property rights and, 144
  quality of, 16, 117
Environmental Protection Agency (EPA), 30
EPIC model, 16
Equity, resources and, 9-12
Erosion, 3, 27
  costs of 29-30, 56-62, 109-110
  as environmental issue, 109-112
  farm structure and, 31-35, 98-100
  off-site impacts, 16, 60-62, 135, 138, 142, 146
  perceptions of, 75, 85-88
  regulation of, 28, 29
  site-specificity, 57
  targeting and, 40-51
  technical assistance and, 71-82
  water-related 83, 109
  (*See also* type of erosion by name)
Erosion control programs. (*See* Conservation programs)
Exchange rates, 18
Experiment stations, state, 138
Exports, 62-63
  assumptions about, 29
Extension services. (*See* Cooperative Extension Service)

Farm(s):
  capital improvements to, 19-20
  family farms, 139
  financial crisis of, 26-27, 31, 36, 112
  income of, 5-7, 11, 22, 97
  leased, 100-105
  mechanization of, 34
  ownership structures, 31-35, 95-106, 139, 149
  (*See also* Land values)
Farmers:
  behavioral change in, 80-81
  characteristics of, 114-118
  conservation adoption by, 19, 108-118, 136, 140-150
  information and, 77-78
  micro-level decisions by, 56-60
  networks of, 78-79, 144
  perceptions of, 75, 80, 85-88

profit motives of, 7, 31, 108-112, 117
property rights of, 4-8, 11, 55, 135, 145
tillage system change and, 59
Farm support programs, 113. (*See also* Subsidies)
Farm bills, 26, 49
Farm Production Economics Survey, 19-20
Farm publications, 74, 78, 90
Farm and ranch directories, 74
Federal government. (*See* Agricultural policy, U.S.)
Federal Water Pollution Control Act Amendments, 28
Fertilizers:
  productivity and, 34-35
  runoff, 28
Funding, constraints, 51

Grass:
  conservation tillage and, 115
  grasslands management, 134

Herbicides, 137. (*See also* Chemicals)
Hunting, 150
Hydrologic response simulation model, 122-123, 148

Incentive programs, 111
  mix of, 136
  (*See also* Subsidies; Tax policies)
Income, farm, 5-7, 11, 22
  cash-flow pressure, 97
  financial crisis in, 26-27, 31, 36, 112
Inflation, 17-18
Information programs:
  access to, 114
  adoption/diffusion model for, 72-82
  changes in, 138
  no-till farming, 89-91
  targeting of, 143-144
  technology transfer, 136
Insecticides, 137. (*See also* Chemicals)
Interest rates, 17-18
  conservation and, 36
  farm income and, 112
  investment and, 21, 23
International trade, 29, 62-63

Irrigation improvements (1971-1984), 19
Land:
  ownership structures, 31-35, 95-106, 139, 146
  property rights, 4-12, 55, 135
  regulation of, 134, 147-148
  rental market, 101
Land values, 36
  adjustments, 20, 22
  conservation and, 5-8, 149
  erosion and, 111
  macro-economic variables, 17-18
  resources and, 9-12
  use regulation, 134, 147-148
Leasing, of farms, 100-105, 146
Legislation, 35
  coordinated, 63
  farm bills, 26, 49
  land retirement, 147-148
  water pollution, 28
  (*See also* Regulation)
Livestock, water fouling and, 87
Local governments:
  agricultural policy and, 63-64
  conservation programs of, 47-51, 147-148
  county centers, 45
  targeting role of, 46

Markets:
  commodities, 32, 35
  farm income and, 5-7, 11, 22, 97
  price supports, 35, 64
  processes, 16-18
Micro-targeting. (*See* Targeting)
Monte Carlo simulation, 123
National Association of Conservation Districts, 48
National Conservation Program, 51
  states' role in, 49
National Resources Inventory (NRI), 3, 63, 96
  Land Ownership Survey, 99
No-till farming, 21, 23, 59-60, 83-92
  income and, 87
  increases in, 137
  user characteristics, 85-89
  yields and, 65, 67-68

Outreach programs, 8. (*See also* Information programs)

Ownership structures, 31-35, 95-106, 146

Pesticides. (*See* Chemicals)

PI model, 16

Pollution:
agricultural, 3, 138
nonpoint, 9-10
(*See also* Water pollution)

Price supports, 35, 64
tax policies and, 113

Productivity, of soil, 19-20, 29
chemical use and, 34-35
erosion and, 57
reduced, 29
survey of, 19-20

Profits. (*See* Cost-benefit analyses)

Property rights, 4-12, 135
compensation and, 11
environmental issues and, 145
marginal benefits and, 55
policy and, 8-12

Public Law 480, 35

Regulation:
erosion and, 28-29
land use, 134, 147-148
SCS and, 30, 37
(*See also* Legislation)

Resources, natural:
equity and, 9-12
governmental intervention and, 15-17
inventory of, 3, 31, 63, 96, 99
management of. (*See* Conservation programs)

Ridge-till systems, 59-60
economic variables in, 67-68
yields and, 65, 67-68

Rill erosion, 12
incidence of, 28-29

Runoff, chemical, 28
off-farm costs, 29

Rural sociology, 27

Salts, 133
runoff, 28
stream-loading, 30

SCS. (*See* Soil Conservation Service)

SEDEC model, 61-62

Sediment:
nonfarm sources, 149

reduction. (*See* Conservation programs)
removal costs, 61, 62-63
sources of, 61

Shadow pricing, 149

Sheet erosion, 12, 28-29

Socioeconomic analyses, 121-128, 140-150

Soil and Water Resources Conservation Act (RCA), 63

Soil conservation districts, 4, 238

Soil Conservation Service (SCS), 7
annual reports, 41
ASCS relations, 42-43, 45
budget reductions, 37
failure of, 56-57
history of, 28-29
as information source, 76-78
no-till survey of, 85
objectives of, 138, 143
regulation and, 30
resource management systems, 150
targeting programs, 40-51

SOILEC model, 61

Soil erosion. (*See* Erosion)

Spring chisel systems, 123-124

Standard Soil Conservation District Law (1937), 4

State governments:
agricultural policy and, 63-64
cost-sharing and, 51
experiment stations, 138
NCP and, 49
targeting role, 46-51

Stripcropping, 146

Subsidies:
comparison of, 127
marginal costs, 57
socioeconomic analysis of, 123-128
tax policy and, 34, 66, 113

Targeting programs, 12, 40-51, 109
analysis of, 123-128
cost comparisons of, 127-128
effectiveness of, 123-125
interorganizational relationships and, 40-51
research on, 134

Tax policies, 18, 134
conservation and, 22-23
as incentives, 66
price supports and, 113
subsidies and, 34

Technical assistance programs, 6, 24,
    111
  as incentive, 136
  targeting of, 40, 46, 123-125
Tennessee Valley Authority (TVA),
    43
Tenure relationships. (*See*
    Ownership structures)
Terraces 64, 147
Tillage clubs, 79, 136
Tillage programs, 21-24, 29, 34
  changes in, 137
  Conservation Tillage Information
    Center, 23, 149
  decision variables, 67
  economics of, 57-60, 99, 125,
    150
  efficiency of, 127-128
  interagency support for, 44
  land tenure and, 105
  micro-targeting, 126
  subsidies for, 123-128
  types of, 115-117
  yields and, 55, 67-68
Tull, Jethro, 137

U.S. Department of Agriculture
    (USDA):
  agency coordination by, 135-136,
    142
  ARS, 40
  ASCS, 85

  centralization trend in, 49
  current policy, 121
  ERS, 20, 40, 137
  farm conservation plans of, 73
  SCS, 7, 28-30, 37, 40-51, 56-57, 76-
    78, 85, 138, 143, 149
  targeting programs, 77
  (*See also* Agricultural policy, U.S.;
    programs by name)
Voluntary compliance programs, 9-
    10, 28-29, 37, 71, 81

Water conservation programs, 62, 66,
    122-128
  public policy and, 26-37
  Soil and Water Resources
    Conservation Act, 63
  (*See also* Conservation programs)
Water erosion, 3, 83, 109
  targeting, 40-51
Water pollution, 9-10, 12, 138
  cost-benefit analysis, 11
  Federal Water Pollution Control
    Act Amendments, 28
  livestock and, 87
  nonpoint, 3, 60-62
  productivity and, 108
Watershed conservation, 62
  policy and, 66, 141
  simulation model for, 122-128, 148
Windbreaks, 64
Wind erosion, 3, 28-29